Left Out!

A Memoir and Other Stories
of Disenfranchised Grief

***

What It Is and
Why It Matters

Left Out!

A Memoir and Other Stories
of Disenfranchised Grief

***

What It Is and
Why It Matters

Norma "Rosie" Wigutoff, MSW

This book contains general information, reflections, exercises, and activities about mental health issues, including grief and loss, depression, anxiety, and shame. Although every effort was made to ensure that the information in this book was correct at press time, it is intended solely for educational purposes and in no way suggests or is a substitute for professional medical, spiritual, religious, or mental health advice, treatment, or therapy. The author and publisher disclaim any liability or responsibility, legal and otherwise, for any loss, disruption, injury, illness, or other damage to persons or property incurred directly or indirectly from applying any of the information in this book. The reader is strongly encouraged to pursue and is responsible for seeking the advice, treatment, and support of their chosen healthcare and spiritual, religious, and mental healthcare providers.

This book is a memoir. It reflects the author's present recollections of experiences over time. Some names and characteristics have been changed, some events have been compressed, and some dialogue has been recreated. Any perceived negative implication of any individual or organization is purely unintentional.

Cover and interior book design by Mi Ae Lipe (whatnowdesign.com).

Cover image by Jason Samadhi (jasonsamadhi.com) with elements generated by OpenAI 4o Image Generator and Firefly 2 Expand, based on the prompt "Create a photorealistic vertical image depicting a quiet, emotionally symbolic outdoor scene," July 15, 2025.

Author photo by Leia Maminta Smith.

Published by Sweet Sea Publications, Seattle, Washington.
Printed in the United States of America.

To contact the author or order additional copies:
Email: normarosie@hotmail.com
Website: Goodwithwords.solutions

Print book ISBN: 979-8-218-72149-7
Library of Congress Control Number: 2025913379

For Kevin, who came to stay,
and to his parents, George and Ann,
who gave this story their blessing.

CONTENTS

PART III | FAMILY STORIES

PART IV | SADIE'S STORY

Don't run from grief, o'soul.
Look for the remedy inside the pain,
Because the rose came from the thorn
And the ruby came from a stone.

—Attributed to Rumi,
thirteenth-century Sufi mystic, poet, and scholar

FOREWORD

WHAT EXACTLY SHOULD A person do when they feel a feeling like grief that the world tells them they aren't supposed to feel? When we're struggling, we're so often told to seek support, but what if the response you get from your support is something along the lines of "You feel THAT about THIS??" What happens if we find ourselves emotionally alone during one of the darkest chapters of our lives?

This isn't a topic that I see many authors willing to address. Although there are many writings on grief, most of them seem to focus on the most typical form of it: the grief we feel when an immediate family member has died. Reading such a book when experiencing a so-called "lesser" form of grief can give the feeling of having accidentally walked into a support group for people with "bigger" problems than you, even if you relate exactly to how they're feeling. Let me say this very clearly: People who are grieving the death of a loved one do not have a monopoly on "grief."

We can grieve the death of our hopes and dreams when we understand that they won't come to fruition. We can grieve the loss of people who are very much still alive, yet no longer a part of our lives. And, as Rosie discusses candidly and in depth, through her own experience of losing her friend, Kevin, we can grieve the loss of those who were not related to us and were in our lives for only a short time. The feelings associated with such losses are no less real than anyone else's.

Grief is a brutal experience even when you're surrounded by understanding, supportive people. The challenge is magnified when those around you simply don't get it. Feelings that are misunderstood, mischaracterized, and invalidated tend to grow in strength and intensity. Unacknowledged grief gets stuck in your chest, growing like a black hole inside of you. You start to wonder if you'll ever feel "normal" again.

There is tremendous power in being able to give a name to an experience. It helps you realize that no matter how alone you feel, you aren't the only person who has ever felt this way. It tells you that someone, somewhere, has probably found a way out of the black hole and through the grief. That's the relief Rosie felt when she learned about disenfranchised grief, and it is the hope she longs to pass on to you through sharing her stories and her strategies.

One of my earliest childhood memories is of a night when I couldn't sleep, tormented by mental images of an act of animal cruelty I had heard of earlier that day. To be clear, I didn't even see this event happen, just heard about it in passing. I heard literally one sentence. I couldn't stop thinking about it. It must have been 2 a.m. when I finally fell asleep. My younger siblings, with whom I shared a room, and who had also heard the story, slept unbothered. I wondered what the hell was wrong with me. I was the oldest one. I was supposed to be the role model, the strong one. Why was I the only member of my family who couldn't handle this?

Reading Rosie's experiences and the reflections she has shared from disenfranchised grief experts felt a bit like gaining access to a secret society I always knew existed, and that I longed for but could never seem to find. Not a dark one, but one that was a sacred sanctuary. Growing up, I often wondered where the other people were who couldn't focus for days or weeks or months when a pet died or when something tragic happened in their periphery. I wondered why everyone seemed so unbothered by what I considered to be terrible losses. I wondered what was wrong with me and if there was anyone else out there like me.

I found one of them, and you'll meet her in this book.

—Dr. Scott Eilers, PsyD, LP
Founder, CEO, Clinical Director, North Star Psychological Center

INTRODUCTION

KEVIN BOGGS DIED on June 6, 2021. He was forty-seven years old. Kevin was not my husband, my lover, my brother, or my yearslong pal. He came to live with me as my tenant, renting the second bedroom in my condo in North Seattle in November 2020 in the midst of the Covid-19 pandemic. We became friends. Seven months later, after being sick for a week, he died. He did not have Covid, and his death was unexpected—and, for me, so was the depth of my grief.

The grief that engulfed me was unimaginable and unendurable. And, as it continued unabated, I could not understand why I still felt so bad, because Kevin was not any of the above to me. He was "just my friend." I grieved, and yet I could not accept it. I was ashamed of it, and I mistrusted it. I could not fathom that my grief over the sudden death of this young man—who had come into my life and then disappeared from it in such a brief time—was as valid and in need of acknowledgment as any other grief. Because of these doubts, I could not surrender to my grief, I could not process it, and I could not heal.

I was in trouble. My heart was broken, but the shame-based, black-and-white-thinking voice in my head started harping at me. "Your grief is not okay, Rosie. You hardly knew Kevin. Get a grip!" Thus, I remained buried under a mountain of discounting messages, complete with shame, confusion, and unrelenting pain, with no way to crawl out from under it and nowhere to go to process it.

Yes, something was wrong. With my thinking, with my pain? Is this too much pain for such a circumstance? Is it simply self-pity? I had no idea. So, I decided to go back to the literature about grief. As a social worker, I had found that turning to literature about life, loss, and grief had served me well over the years, with my clients and myself—in any mental, emotional, or spiritual crisis.

When I happened upon a fascinating online video called "Disenfranchised Grief: Dr. Ken Doka," I thought, *Hmmm...interesting title*. In the interview, Dr. Kenneth J. Doka, PhD, a professor of gerontology, a prolific author and speaker, and a leading authority on grief, death, and dying, describes how, in the 1980s, he came up with the term for experiences of grief that his graduate students were describing in class—grief that they and their patients did not feel they had a right to, or that, despite their pain, was invalidated, disenfranchised by society. It struck Doka that the word *disenfranchised* perfectly described these kinds of grief; they are buried and hidden, a limitless, unexplored host of grief experiences that fall outside society's norms of what is "real grief."[1]

That was my eureka moment.

Okay, I thought. *That sounds exactly right. That sounds just like me... feeling like I don't have the right to grieve over Kevin! So, it has a name! It's called disenfranchised grief. What a great term. Yes, that's it! It's still grief.* As I watched this video, I felt like shouting the news from the rooftops. And so, I began to do just that. Then, when everyone said, "What? Hey, I can relate to that! That's called disenfranchised grief? Wow...what a relief!"—the idea for this book was born.

***

As we are aware, certain kinds of loss and grief are well known and well defined. This is the kind of grief that I affectionately call "grief with a capital G." This is the grief we all speak of as the most brutal and difficult to bear, the grief we agree to make room for, at least for a while, such as the long-awaited—or sudden—death of an aged and beloved spouse, the traumatic and unexpected death of a young spouse, the death of a parent, a sibling, or worst of all, the death of a child. Certainly, this is all true grief and is so easily identified. It is true for anyone who has endured one of these most brutal of losses.

And then, there are the other kinds of grief and loss that don't count as grief with a capital G for you and me. They might include something like the death of a friend or an ex-husband you divorced years ago. Or, perhaps it was the death of a neighbor's cat, or their little dachshund you adored that moved away—or the hummingbird with the iridescent purple throat you'd been watching for weeks that had been drunkenly sucking nectar from your hummingbird feeder and that you recently found lying belly-up on the floor of the deck, as cold and still as a stone. Or something huge, but too far away to matter to you and me, such as the loss of the rainforests; the sharp increase in natural disasters, wars, and starving children in faraway countries; and the instability and chaos of governments, including our own. Like the too-big and too-small beds in the three bears' house, such grief is not comfortable. It doesn't fit us. These situations don't count as grief that should break our own tender hearts.

Last, but not least, there are the universal, limitless, subtle, and often not-even-so-subtle kinds of loss that we tend to lump together under the definition of "life passages," rather than grief. We nod knowingly: losing our first tooth or favorite stuffed bear; waving goodbye to our bigger humans as we climb aboard the school bus to go to kindergarten for the first time; leaving home for college or marriage or a place of our own; losing a job; getting a divorce; losing the family home; getting sick; getting wrinkles; and, if we are lucky, growing, if not wiser, at least older.

These life passages happen every day. We think about them, talk about them, deal with them, analyze them, agonize over them, meditate on them, and survive them. Whew! They are the inevitable and sometimes not-so-inevitable footsteps along our life's journey, but more often than not—we do *not* think about them in terms of real grief at all. Maybe, when we reach the point where it looks like we are not going to survive these passages, we might then give ourselves the luxury of thinking about them as "real grief," but sometimes not even then. They're "just life."

When such losses, from the neighbor's pet to these "life passages" that all humans endure, are causing us pain, but we do not recognize and acknowledge them as our grief, or as grief at all, we have no way to begin to heal them. But, when we can say "This is grief," "This is my grief," and "I'm sad!" we have the opportunity to respond to the hurt, to tend to and heal it, to take inner and outer action as we carry such grief with us lovingly throughout our lives. This, dear reader, is what this book is about.

***

In recent years, grief experts like Doka have begun talking more about disenfranchised grief, sometimes calling it hidden grief, hidden sorrow, and neglected grief among other terms. Many people have never heard of any of these terms. I certainly hadn't when Kevin died. The term *disenfranchised grief* pretty much covers all these other kinds of grief—except for the worst kind, the grief with a capital G.

In sum, disenfranchised grief is when a person is denied—either by themselves or others (whether it is family, friends, community, larger society, or all the above)—their right to acknowledge, validate, and attend with love to their grief. It happens when society tells us that if our grief is not as bad as someone else's, it does not count and therefore it must be diminished, set aside, or shamed. Yes, it so often happens with those "other people's grief" and "life passages" too. And, sadly, even the worst kind of grief often eventually becomes disenfranchised in our Western society.

It is true, and reassuringly so, that when we compare our grief to that of others—"My grief is bad, but it's just not that bad compared to yours"—it can indeed be a good thing, an acknowledgment that lets us feel grateful. Nevertheless, such a comparison can throw us down and out like a boxer left gutted by a knock-out punch. Because, when we compare our grief to that of another at the expense of our own, when we minimize, discount, and shame our own grief, that act—and I believe, the shame most of all—can make us sick—literally sick—in our bodies, minds, and spirits.

Let's take a brief look at the emotion of shame before we move on. You might know well the feeling, "I could have died of shame." Whether or not we have committed some awful act, we feel smaller than the smallest snail and wish desperately to crawl into some dark hole in the earth and disappear. As defined by Merriam-Webster:

Shame *(noun)*
1a : a painful emotion caused by consciousness of
        guilt, shortcoming, or impropriety…
1b : the susceptibility to such emotion
2 : a condition of humiliating disgrace or disrepute
Synonym examples: remorse, regret, guilt

(verb)
1 : to bring shame to : disgrace
Synonym examples: humiliate, embarrass, disgrace[2]

Phrases containing *shame*: a crying shame, body-shame, put (someone or something) to shame, shame on (someone), hang one's head in shame

The list goes on. This is not a good feeling.

Thus, the task is clear—it is vital and imperative that we tend with great care, especially to the shame associated with disenfranchised grief. The experts say so, and I agree. This is worth repeating and is a major message of this book. We can acknowledge, validate, honor, and engage with our shame and our grief gently and self-compassionately. Such loving attention does not let the shame or the grief rule us. We are not giving in to it. It is part of the work we must do along the healing journey.

***

Inside the pages of this book, you will discover the story of Kevin and me and my grief over his loss, how I discovered the term *disenfranchised grief,* and my one-day-at-a-time journey of learning how to reenfranchise and embrace that grief. You will also find other real-life stories about who and what we love, lose, and grieve, and our right to love and grieve all of it, no matter how "invalid" or "insignificant" or "too far away" the grief—or the love—may seem to others, and even to ourselves.

I offer this book to you as a self-compassionate road map—a beginner's how-to guide of sorts—to help you recognize when you are experiencing feelings of shame, self-loathing, or other distressing emotions that might mean you have a whopping case of disenfranchised grief. It is a guide for how to learn to acknowledge and engage with our grief, no matter how illegitimate it may feel.

Although these stories of disenfranchised grief are, of course, like in every love story, as unique to each griever as are our fingerprints, I believe they all have one thing in common. This one thing is shame. The shame, the hiding, and the secrecy, conscious or not, is the biggest threat to our grief work and grief healing. The shame—the humiliation, disgrace, and isolation we feel when we are left out of society's grief rituals, condolences, connections, and traditions, cause deep, universal, and unnecessary suffering for our minds, our bodies, and our souls. This shame is what I hope people will begin to free themselves from over time, as they allow themselves to practice grieving openly and in community—to know that it is okay to acknowledge and validate the shame and the rejected or neglected grief; to engage with all these feelings with reverence, curiosity, tenderness, and love; and to receive the crucial and necessary support from others that we have a right to, as sentient beings who are designed for communion and community. This is the way that disenfranchised grief becomes visible, the way that it takes its rightful place alongside all grief, and then becomes disenfranchised no more.

So, dear reader: This book is my love letter, my ode, to Kevin and disenfranchised grievers everywhere. If you find in these pages a story, a quote, or a snippet of information that resonates with you or guides you, something relevant to you, someone you know, or someone you have never met and never will, but whose story moves you just the same, I hope you will let me know; or perhaps share it with a trusted person. Indeed, we are all a part of this larger love story and this community of disenfranchised grievers because we are all disenfranchised grievers at some point in our lives.

So let us dive in.

Part I

***

Kevin's Story

CHAPTER ONE

Prelude to Grief

ON THE TWENTY-THIRD of May 1976, I graduated from the Boston University School of Social Work with my master's degree. I was an eager, optimistic, smart, feminist, middle-class, twenty-six-year-old single Jewish woman. I had worked hard, I was thrilled with and proud of my degree, and I was eager to "officially" begin saving and changing lives.

And I loved living in Boston. Over the years, I went from being a hospital social worker, mostly helping families find nursing homes for their elderly relatives who sat groaning lethargically in wheelchairs in hospital corridors, to working at Catholic Charities with families referred through protective services and unwed pregnant teenage girls trying to decide whether to keep or surrender their babies-to-be. Then I went on to work at an organization where I matched kids who needed "big brothers" and "big sisters" with young adults who wanted to *be* "big brothers" and "big sisters." And finally, after a move to Seattle in 1987, I started my flourishing private practice in counseling. I fell in love (in a good way!) with all—or at least most—of my clients.

Then, beginning in 1999, I morphed from being a therapist in private practice to being a private eldercare companion, caring for amazing "little ol' ladies" mostly in their eighties and nineties. A couple of years after being thrown into the deep end as a newbie caregiver whose job was to tend primarily (and kindly, of course) to my clients' optimal physical well-being and safety, it dawned on me that I was blossoming into much more than that. That enhanced role was what I later came to call myself a "therapeutic eldercare companion"—with the accompanying title, higher pay, and an equally enhanced sense of professional self-esteem. Now, my focus went beyond tending to my clients' physical well-being to fostering an overall nurturing, high-quality relationship—one that increased my clients' overall sense of emotional and mental well-being.

I fell in love with these clients, too (or mostly all of them), and when each one inevitably died within two or three or four years of my meeting them, I missed them and was sad, of course. But they were not my real family, nor were their families and their pets. These losses were not as bad for me, I told myself. I concentrated on being grateful for the mutually nurturing and tender times I had spent with them.

Of course, I had my fair share of big life changes and personal losses over all those years, including some that, as I got older, I perceived and could take credit for as rightfully "mine," as grief with a capital G. I was smart and introspective enough, even in my late teens and twenties, to get into therapy and was glad and grateful to continue on and off forever over one "issue" or another.

***

How had I gotten here? I was an adorable, doe-eyed, petite, poised, and ponytailed (and popular with the boys!) grade-schooler until about the age of eleven. Somehow, I was then abruptly and unceremoniously transformed into an "ugly duckling," going-into-junior-high kid with ugly glasses, acne, and a raging case of debilitating shyness, wearing a scratchy, too-tight elasticized panty girdle to school (all of us girls wore them in those days, whether we needed to or not! We, assuredly, did not). By high school, I was anything *but* cheerleader material and the popular girls made sure I knew it. I felt left out, lonely, and ashamed, and my only sibling, David, who was brilliant, introverted, and three and a half years older than me, pretty much ignored me too. To describe this as an excruciating time for me would be an understatement.

The door into a social and intellectual world finally began to slowly creak open for me when I went off to college at American University in Washington, DC, and for the first time lived away from home. I lived in Anderson Hall, the girls' dormitory. (In those days, girls' dorms and boys' dorms were in separate buildings, complete with 11 p.m. curfews on weeknights and midnight on the weekends, with sign-in sheets and demerits for being late. And when a boy visited a girl in her dorm room, the door had to remain open. If a visitor was sitting on the bed, they had to have one foot on the floor at all times!) All these life changes, new experiences, and emotions made good fodder for therapy, but I never thought about them as grief. It was simply life and about growing up and becoming a psychologically "fit, productive, and happy" adult female human. It was all about those persnickety but unavoidable life passages. I majored in psychology. It was fascinating.

These life passages and transitions continued to come fast and furiously, with the inevitable, typical ups and downs of finding my way in higher academia, in the big city, and in the world. After my sophomore year, I moved off-campus into a two-bedroom apartment with another girl—mainly so I could adopt my first cat, the kitten named Cruella De Vil. (More on her later.) No pets were allowed in the dorms, so having my first, a frisky little female kitten, was a dream come true, but living with that particular female human roommate, not so much. It was a learning experience, though, and I learned a great deal.

A couple of years later, once I graduated from college with a bachelor's degree in psychology and had had enough of that particular kind of life learning, I found my very own first apartment, a small daylight-basement studio in an old but elegant, well-maintained brick building called the Copley Plaza. It was called the Copley Courts when it was built in 1916 and stood in the heart of Dupont Circle in what was, during my time there, a funky, hippie-inhabited mecca. The studio rented for a whopping $150 a month—whopping at the time.

I settled into my young-adult life as a twenty-something woman living alone with her cat in the nation's capital city. I worked several interesting jobs during that time, mostly secretarial, while I was busily figuring out what I was going to do with the rest of my life. I knew it would have something to do with psychology and helping people.

My first was being the personal secretary to the mild-mannered, slight-of-build, brilliant, and bespectacled Bill Cherkasky, the administrative assistant to Senator Gaylord Nelson. Senator Nelson was the dashing and equally kind senior US senator from Wisconsin who had been that state's thirty-fifth governor and was best known for being the founder of Earth Day. I got the job by walking confidently through the halls of the Old Senate Office Building (built in 1909 and originally called the Senate Office Building, but when a second building was constructed in 1958, it took on its elder statesman moniker); I placed cold-call knocks on the doors of any Democratic senator whose staff might be looking for a smart, young, capable secretary. I was such a person, college-educated, eager, and wanting to make my first real money and my first real mark in the world. Bill Cherkasky agreed. Landing that job was a coup, and the salary was also whopping at the time, $7,000 a year! And I found Tom, my latest cute, smart, and funny boyfriend. Finding boyfriends was a pretty easy thing to do once I started college. It was a rich time in my life in more ways than just my salary.

Since finishing college, I had been researching graduate school programs in psychology and social work when I discovered the Master of Social Work programs at both Boston University and Simmons College. Neither school required math and statistics, subjects that were part of most four-year, PhD-level psychology curricula—subjects I had always loathed. I applied.

When I was accepted to BU's School of Social Work for the fall of 1974 (I was thrilled that I was also accepted to Simmons, but was put on their waitlist because they had no room for that year—but yay for me!), I accepted BU's offer. I said good-bye to Tom (who I found out had recently been cheating on me anyway). I tried hard to feel mad about that news but felt mostly sweaty and sick to my stomach and could barely eat for a while—but no sense in grieving any of that—he had been a pretty darn-good beau while it lasted, I had to admit. I packed a small U-Haul rental truck with my stuff, loaded my car with Cruella and some plants, and drove to Beantown for my next big adventure. Tom drove the U-Haul. Yeah, Tom, the very same. I know. It was complicated.

Boston fit me like a glove, and I stayed for thirteen years. As I've mentioned, graduate school brought me deep social, collegial, and academic satisfaction, and it flung open an even wider door into a rewarding career as a social worker. My various social work jobs were deeply gratifying. I worked hard, traveled once or twice a year for fun (including my favorites, France and Mexico), and I had my dear women friends. There were dating diversions, dilemmas and disasters, boyfriends, and other romantic ups and downs, but nothing that led to my longed-for goal of marriage with my soulmate.

Life was good. In the early 1980s, I became a first-time homeowner of a lovely, century-old brownstone condominium in Brighton that my dad helped me finance. I had my work, friends, the inscrutable and now elegantly aging Cruella, and my favorite haunts in the city. But, at last, by the late '80s, I felt it was time to move on again, and I had good reasons. Boston's housing costs—especially for a thirty-something single professional woman with no 401(k)—were rising sharply; its frigid, icy winters were getting icier and frigider (is that even a word?); and the city's once-vast sea of suitable soulmate fish had shrunk into a scant, dried-up puddle of emaciated, unreliable brown toads. I had kissed enough of them. I was ready for another chapter, another challenge, another life passage transition.

I buckled down to the requisite research again and discovered the warmer, greener, friendlier, and less expensive climes of Seattle, Washington, the aptly nicknamed "Emerald City" of the Pacific Northwest. In the spring of 1987, I sold the brownstone for a healthy profit; that summer, before I left Beantown, I began drum set lessons, visualizing myself as Ringo Starr, my favorite Beatle. That, and a brief, torrid affair with my hunky, twenty-something drum teacher, did a brilliant job of distracting me from the stress of the impending move. Anyway, there really wasn't that much to be stressed or sad *about*. I was beginning another new adventure. I was excited!

***

Thus, that fall, at the age of thirty-seven, I put most of my worldly belongings in storage and left the now sweet-sixteen Cruella safely ensconced with a farming couple south of Boston who fostered elderly and ailing cats. Then I set off on my first-ever cross-country road trip, driving my nifty silver Toyota Celica with race-car pop-up headlights. The adventure was purposely leisurely and took seven weeks. When I arrived in Seattle, something clicked. I knew I had reached the Emerald City and my sought-after rainbow, my heaven on earth with its black pot spilling over with gold. The majestic snow-capped Olympic Mountains to the west and the Cascades to the east, which I could see almost every day from anywhere in the city, convinced me. I have lived in Seattle ever since.

I settled in and similarly recreated my life. I found more dear girlfriends, a few more short-term secretarial jobs to get by, and then, fulfilling my career heart's goals, I found gratifying social work jobs. With the proceeds from the sale of the Boston brownstone, I purchased a modest condo in a neighborhood of mostly Victorian houses on Seattle's upper Capitol Hill. And, when I was ready, I set up my private practice as a therapist. When Cruella finally died at the very old age of twenty, I cried every day at first. But I had much more cat love in my heart to offer, and a few weeks after I lost Cruella, I adopted a new kitty, Sweet Pea.

And, life went on. In 1991, with the availability of suitable husbands-to-be becoming as slim as back East, I bought my first cute little white-brick, stand-alone house in a small northeast Seattle neighborhood. It boasted two medium-sized bedrooms, an ample living room with a fireplace, a huge kitchen, and an office in the back. There was a gently sloping backyard with a glorious old weeping willow tree at the edge of the property bordering the woods and a two- or three-postage-stamp–sized, easy-to-mow front yard with several rose bushes climbing along a rustic wood fence. I didn't mind mowing the front yard in the summer; I had my dad's housewarming gift of a fancy new gas-powered lawn mower. The sloping backyard, I didn't worry about as much, since even the gently sloping part was too much sloping for me and the gas-guzzling mower.

CHAPTER TWO

Hello, Grief with a Capital G

As they inevitably do, my first serious grief-with-a-capital-G experiences, as I understood them at the time, began to present themselves. Not just typical "life passages," but hard-core, real grief. One of the first events to register high on my personal Richter earthquake–magnitude scale of grief occurred in October 1997, less than a month before my forty-eighth birthday. It was the sudden death of my dear ol', emotionally softened and formerly grouchy dad. I had been in Seattle for ten years.

My parents had retired to Sun City, Arizona, in 1972, the year I graduated from college, and they had been happily ensconced there ever since. Now, four months after Dad died, a few days after Valentine's Day in 1998, Mom died too—also suddenly. Well, you can imagine that was big-time grief, losing both parents within four months of each other. That qualified as grief with a capital G, *right*? It was the kind of double-whammy loss I had no problem claiming as mine.

But, as I mourned, I gradually became aware of some subtle grief warnings roiling around in the societal atmosphere, such as "appropriate markers" for grief, how long one should grieve, how deeply one should grieve, and even what that grief should look and feel like! (Put a pin in that for more in Chapter Eleven.) But at that time, those rules about grief—rules that were *not* clearly defined—contained rigid lines in the sand that I learned a person crossed at their own risk. The punishments, however, were clear, and I knew I must avoid them, but following the rules was tricky. Like walking among unexploded bombs in a minefield, I was not sure where and what they were, and how to avoid them.

I read books, went to therapy, and listened to people talk about what grief is like when you become an orphan in your late forties. It was hard but doable, and there was always room for gratitude amid the sadness. My parents were both eighty-two years old when they died; they had lived good, long lives and had been so happily married, everyone said. This was true, and they were still madly in love with each other after all those years, right up until the very end. Also true. I could be grateful they were together again and at peace now. *So, luckily for me*, I thought, *I don't have to grieve too desperately or for too long. I will be okay. I will be fine.*

It was *also* true that my relationships with both my parents had been a little complicated growing up, so that made the grief a little complicated too. Mom had been a loving but stereotypically smothering, overprotective Jewish mom (no offense to the many magnificent Jewish moms out there, of whom I have known many) until I was about twelve; up to that point, we were close. But, once that teenage milestone came and went, she and I pretty much never again saw eye to eye about anything. Hardly anything I did was the right thing, or the "good enough" thing, *especially* when it was something I wanted to have, or wanted to do, and with which she disagreed. Except, thankfully, for politics, where there was never any disagreement. We were all devoted Democrats in my family. Who wasn't in love with John F. Kennedy?

So, as I became a teenager, Mom transformed into what I came to think of as the ice queen, someone more akin to one of those wicked witches straight out of one of the Brothers Grimm's fairy tales or the Wizard of Oz than a *real* mother. Her tactic when she disapproved of my brother's or my behavior—and very occasionally Dad's—was to freeze us out. It was quite a wind chill. She did not yell or sit us down for long, earnest talks or angry lectures. Instead, she would silently turn her witheringly cold look our way, then turn her back and walk out of whatever room we were in, leaving us stricken and stunned but not surprised. And the older I got, the icier she became. Sometimes I would yell at her, but any response was short and curt and she *never, ever* raised her voice. There was mostly just "the look."

And Dad, as you know, was like me—or I was like Dad—since we both wore our emotions, joy, sadness, anger, and frustration on our sleeves. In those days (and even before I was in my "terrible teens"), he was mostly angry all the time; he would yell about everything and nothing and was generally not a pleasant person to be around. There was never any physical discipline, though. That was a cardinal rule in our home. That was a good thing, and I am glad of it.

But, while their disciplinary styles were different, Mom and Dad were a united front, and the atmosphere at home growing up was usually either hot or cold—Mom's blistering cold and Dad's piping hot—interspersed with the rare "I love you, sweetie" or "I'm proud of you" moments for the perfect behavior my brother and I were always striving so anxiously to achieve. It was disconcerting and kept us off-balance. One emotion, though, that I don't remember ever seeing Mom express was sadness. Except once. Dad had yelled at her, and later I hugged her around the waist while she cried.

But, hey—both my parents were gone now, and all that stress and conflict was over. I reminded myself of this often, and so did everyone else. It was in the past, and I could forgive them, everyone said. *Okay, got it*, I thought. *That sounds like a good plan.* Every five minutes or so, I reminded myself, *It isn't so bad. Losing one's parents, even so close together, it's all part of life. Others have had it so much worse. I'll get over it. I can forgive them now for not being perfect parents.* So, I did my best to "do my grief right" and "process" my complicated feelings and forgive them the way I was told—the way I knew. And I had therapy to help me. That would get me through these particularly traumatic times. At that time, it did. Life was good, mostly; it truly was. I even had a nice Jewish boyfriend then and that helped too. He supported me in my grief. The inevitable ups and downs and the flow of life continued, and I felt lucky.

***

In the fall of 1999, about a year and a half after Dad and Mom died, *he* happened! My soulmate arrived. I had ditched the nice Jewish boyfriend, who, although he was nice, was chronically depressed and not emotionally available, to put it mildly. And, finally, if you're keeping track, you'll know it was then—*after* my parents died—that *he* showed up in my life. It would take more time in therapy to figure out why that was significant. To be truthful, I'm still working on it, but I think I have it mostly figured out.

Yes, dear reader, my husband-to-be had been, as they say, literally only a stone's throw away. When I moved into my first little house in North Seattle in 1991, Charles, the aforementioned *he*, was living catty-corner across the street from me in his own little house with his four-year-old daughter, Brianna, and his toddler son, Eli. I had known him all this time simply as my tall, blond, lean, dreamily handsome, and always happily helpful neighbor; he had a tall, blond, willowy, and equally amiable girlfriend named Fran. Charles broke up with Fran around the time I was grieving my parents. We started to talk in our neighborly, across-the-fence way about our losses. He spoke candidly, and he was a good listener. And, he was so handsome.

By the fall of 1999, our easy friendship had developed into one of genuine confidants. And I guess I fell in love. So, I decided to take a chance, knowing that it might not be wise, and I would be completely vulnerable. One afternoon in November, with poorly disguised casualness, I ran across the street, found Charles at home, and spilled it. I told him I had a crush on him. Well, to my utter surprise, he said he had a crush on me too. And from there, it went fast. We became inseparable, which was convenient, thanks to the proximity of our houses. By February 2000, we were talking marriage, and by spring, we were planning the wedding. Finally (*"finally,"* as my brother said sarcastically during his after-dinner toast at our wedding at a small Victorian inn on Lopez Island), those welcome wedding bells rang (metaphorically speaking). The day was October 28, 2000, just a blink of an eye before I turned fifty-one years old. Charles was fifty-four.

Charles and I had sold our respective little houses and together we bought a larger one where we'd be a family and where his kids, then thirteen and ten, could do their weekly back-and-forth living rotation between our house and their mom and stepdad's. Charles was the best husband. He was my dream come true, my soulmate, indeed my "last and forever-lasting true love," and we were happy. He did most of the cooking, he read to me in bed at night, he wrote me love notes in the mornings, and he kissed me often. He created lush gardens in the previously plain front and backyards; he stripped the paint off the walls on either side of the living room fireplace to reveal gorgeous wood paneling. We went on long walks and never stopped talking. Well, we didn't talk so much when the kids were there, but we made do. He adored me, and I adored him. I was safe now. He would be my only and forever husband. (As it has turned out, at least through the writing of this book, he has still been my only husband. And that's okay.)

Our marriage lasted three years. There was just one reason why I got out; it was a doozy and happened without warning. It turns out that Charles had been draining money from his kids' college trust fund for years to buy drugs for the heroin habit he had developed as a helicopter pilot in the Vietnam War. He had finally gotten clean a few years before I met him, but the money pilfering from the trust fund had continued. I knew all about his drug history and that he was clean when we met, but I had known nothing about the money.

Charles confessed to me one balmy afternoon in late September, when we were all still in post-9/11 shock. He got home from work and asked me to come sit in his van with him. And then he told me. His ex-wife had recently checked the balance in the trust fund account after ignoring it for ages and had found it almost at zero. He admitted to her that he had taken it—a few dollars here and a few dollars there, intending (as addicts always do) the whole time to redeposit it. She told him he would have to pay it all back now or go to jail. You can imagine September was not a good month that year.

And that was it. In one short sentence, a rogue wave of words broke over our marriage and swept it away. We spent our second year of marriage packing and then preparing and selling the house. During the third year, we lived apart, went to marriage counseling (which quickly morphed into divorce counseling), and finally filed for divorce.

In June 2003, Charles and I signed divorce papers in a judge's chambers in downtown Seattle. Afterward, we went out to breakfast together to celebrate how amicable our divorce process had been. It mostly was. God, what a relief.

Yes, I grieved—a lot—but I was encouraged not to wallow. I was still stunned, and I was angry, so very angry. His betrayal had been unexpected and egregious. And, I was so deeply, bitterly disappointed. But

I was lucky I had dodged what could have been a much more exquisite-ly painful bullet. *Imagine how awful it would have been if you'd found out after you were married for years! Or imagine if he had cheated on you, or started using again,* my friends told me. I agreed. *And thank God you had your prenup!* It was all true. Sad, but true. I got back into therapy.

***

By the time Charles and I were divorced, I was also dealing with the gnawing (and nagging) fact that I had never birthed a child, and it was too late by that time. You might recall that I was in the last week of my fiftieth year when I married, and I fantasized about being on the cover of *Newsweek* as one of the oldest first-time moms in US history. It did not happen, no surprise. That was sad, of course.

But my friends also often reminded me how hard parenting was and how lucky I was that I did not have to deal with any of that life-long worry and heartache that kids inevitably bring. *And remember those stepkids you had to put up with when you were married!* (Well, yes. Brianna, at thirteen, had been blasé about the marriage and about me; she had her own friends, and she and I got along pretty well. But Eli was not happy with my intrusion into his established family's world, from the day Charles and I became a couple to the day we parted. Eli was a bright, handsome, athletic, and funny kid, but, oh, what a tough cookie he was with me.) *All that was hard enough,* my friends said. *Imagine if you had had children together, and one of them had become a drug addict and, God forbid, died of an overdose or committed suicide.* I should feel grateful for all those things that had *not* happened. And, at the time, I mostly did feel grateful—except when I was consumed by devastation, betrayal, and loneliness.

Sometimes now, decades later, I still think fleetingly about the abortion I had at six weeks along when I was twenty-four years old. The pregnancy was ectopic. My medical insurance did not cover abortions at the time, even for ectopic pregnancies. (I don't remember if that was really the case or not, but it must have been because I remember having to pay for the procedure out of pocket.) My boyfriend Tom went with me to the Planned Parenthood clinic in Washington, DC. Even if the pregnancy had been viable, we were not ready for a baby at our age, life circumstances, and our relationship status (we were not a forever-committed couple). Tom and I never talked about it afterward, and I never told more than a couple of close friends. It was our private business and not a topic of casual conversation. And I knew that this loss did not compare to losing an actual real live *baby*.

So, yes, I know it's okay to have grieved that loss then and to grieve it still. I wonder what that baby would have been like if it *had* been viable, if it would have been a boy or a girl, if it would have lived and grown to adulthood and had a good life, and what kind of relationship we would have had. When I do think about it, the yearning comes. I always imagine a girl. She is always a girl.

***

So, on a sunny Seattle day that June 2003, the day after I became a brand-new, first-time divorcée, I moved into my spacious, cozy, fifteen-hundred-square-foot, two-bedroom, two-bath condominium unit in a brand-new, three-story building in a small, modest neighborhood in North Seattle. It was perfect. Not a speck of dust anywhere, except for maybe a little sawdust left over from the new construction. The primary bedroom suite was roomy, with a private bathroom that sported two sinks and long countertops, and was large enough to dance a waltz in. Who needs a bathroom that big, even with a litterbox? *Nice for a couple*, I thought, feeling jealous of no one. You could walk straight through the bathroom and into an even bigger walk-in closet. I chose it as the guestroom suite and took the smaller back bedroom for myself because it was even quieter and overlooked a bucolic green space outside the window. The view transported me out of my urban surroundings into what reminded me of a wildflower-swept Provençal countryside scene. And who needed double sinks? Not me.

Life trundled along. I continued my "loving-care companion relationships" with my adored and adorable little old ladies; I enjoyed long, deep talks, laughs, cries, and adventures with my girlfriends; I dated more frogs, a scallywag or two, and a couple of almost-princes; I read, journaled, worked out at the gym, and attended movies, the ballet, and musical theatre; I continued to be a cat mom to Sweet Pea; and I went to therapy.

About five years later, in 2008, I began renting out the primary bedroom suite, once I had sufficiently recuperated from a stroke I had in January 2007. I was extremely lucky with the stroke. It was mild, attacking only the language centers of my brain and leaving me with all my physical abilities intact. The hint of hesitation here and there with my speech was remedied with a few sessions of speech therapy and about six months of taking it easy, doctor's orders.

To be sure, the stroke left me a little stunned and a little traumatized; it was a big surprise to have any kind of stroke—even a mild one—at the age of fifty-seven. But I was lucky, everyone said. And I was. Lucky and grateful. So that was how I mostly felt. Grief, yeah, a little, but mostly lucky and relieved and grateful.

And, the fact that just a few weeks after the stroke, I flew to Morelia, the capital of Michoacán in Mexico and a UNESCO World Heritage Site, and hung out for four months while I investigated possible expat dream haunts doesn't mean I wasn't taking it easy. The beloved Sweet Pea had died a few months earlier at the age of nineteen and a half, and I had already planned this trip, booked a flight, and, with the help of a welcoming Mexican real estate agent named Marisol, had reserved a place to stay in a cozy two-bedroom, two-story apartment smack-dab in the middle of the historic downtown.

The historic town center is famous for its grand Spanish-style architecture, built almost entirely from the pale pink–hued volcanic stone called *cantera rosa* (quarry rose) that was dug from the city's nearby hills during the mid-sixteenth through the nineteenth century. I had been dreaming of this town of dusty-rose light, and I was medically forbidden to drive for six months anyway, so what the heck? My doctor okayed the trip, so off I flew to the land of cantera rosa, handsome policía turística, chicken mole, and Frida Kahlo. Who knew who and what I might discover there? (In fact, I did discover a handsome tourist policeman who became my companion for most of those months…but that's for another story.)

Once I got home from Morelia and settled back into life in Seattle, I lost no time in adopting Sadie Grace, my third kitty companion. She was a shy, petite, two-year-old, long-haired dilute tortie with a luxurious variegated coat of gray, brown, and mocha and a regal skyward-strutting tail as fluffy as caramel cotton candy.

I returned to my caregiving and began the search for a good renter for the primary bedroom suite. I definitely could use the rental income, and besides, because of the stroke, I did not want to live alone anymore. God forbid, I should have another stroke, or stumble in the night, hit my head, and die. If something awful like that happened, I didn't need a best friend around—just a friendly, clean, and cooperative tenant who would find my body sooner rather than later. And, living alone was lonely. I felt better having an amiable face around for a bit of social intercourse once or twice a day.

So, I put an ad on Craigslist. Nothing could go awry with *that* plan, surely.

CHAPTER THREE

Life Before Kevin—
the Quest for the Essential Roomie

IT WAS THE FALL of 2020, and the pandemic had been well underway since the previous March. I had just turned seventy-one. I had lived and loved, suffered and survived, moved and married, and divorced and moved again. I had grieved and grown. I had worked, read, and studied; taken continuing education courses and kept up with the latest theories on psychology, human behavior, death and dying, spirituality, and the Buddhist approach to all of it; and had tenants good, bad, and ugly. And I stuck with my own therapy.

I was sure I knew more than enough about grief and loss to last me the rest of my present lifetime, and that I had this "grief thing" down. I had been "doing it right"—for myself and with my clients. I knew there was big, bad grief, and there was occasional medium-sized, time-limited, not-so-big-and-bad grief, and then there was everything else: yearning, missing, anger, anxiety, moving, illness, betrayal, and aging—including the betrayal *of* aging. All that life transition stuff. Sad, but not really grief.

Sadly, here I was, still single, more than seventeen years since my divorce. But I thought I was still pretty cute, still young at heart and in every other way for my age. My big brown eyes still twinkled. My still petite, five-foot-almost-one-inch frame, my waistline, and biceps were all in good order. And my stylish, pixie brunette head of hair, sprinkled now with silvery gray, remained still mostly on my head. After all, they say that seventy is the new fifty, right?

So, I still had high hopes for my second and this-time-everlasting soulmate's impending arrival. But I still could not find him (*What is that about?* I wondered every day), with lately not even a likely suspect for a third, second, or even a first date. And yes, that is despite the myriad "silver singles–style" online dating sites (yes, I'd tried them all… well, almost, except for the hard-core ones). I also endured the occasional blind date through a friend (you don't want to get me started) and even contemplated hanging out in the organic produce section of Trader Joe's, fondling the cantaloupe and hoping for the best. I tried it more than a few times; it never worked.

And—ta da!—I was looking for a new tenant again. As I have mentioned, things had been up and down on that front, and in recent years more down than up. Let me tell you about some of those experiences. You might not believe these stories, but they are all true, I promise. This is nonfiction, remember. They give you a feel for the vital importance, the potential pitfalls and fallout, the good and bad, and the delicate, tricky, and complex business of finding the "essential roomie."

I know what you might be thinking: *Well, duh! You kept putting ads on Craigslist! Are you out of your mind?* Okay, I hear you. But hold on.

***

Over the first dozen years or so of renting out the big bedroom, some of my tenants were indeed friendly, clean, and cooperative. Some even became dear and lasting friends. Others, not so much. One tenant was so quiet that I hardly knew he was there. That was fine. Another tenant, Max, a funny and brilliantly talented theatre actor, created an audiobook recording studio in the huge walk-in closet, complete with soundproofing, and gave me free tickets to all his first-night performances. That was cool. But there was the time, early on, when I discovered that he had broken one of my dinner plates, and, instead of telling me, he hid the pieces at the bottom of the kitchen trash. It wasn't hard to discover them because they rattled. Even so, Max stayed for four years. Other than the broken china, he was mostly okay, and I was forgiving. Most tenants were about average on the good-tenant scale and stayed six months to a year, and sometimes two or three.

My very first tenant was Eddie, a tall, string-bean-thin, shy, pleasant-mannered single man in his mid-thirties. Eddie always dressed in flannels and baggy, worn, but clean jeans. The poor guy had terrible teeth and even more terrible grammar, but he was awfully nice. He had just moved to Seattle and found work as a marine electrician for Argosy Cruises, the tour boat company on Lake Union in downtown Seattle. He was quiet, kept mostly to himself, and didn't have many belongings—some clothes, a few paperback books, a couple of frayed bath towels, and other sundries. But he was friendly and accommodating, and he was thrilled to be in charge of feeding Sadie dinner, now that I was going back to work and sometimes wasn't home till late. Eddie liked Sadie and was very good with her, and she seemed to like him too.

Things went well at first. What I did not know was that Eddie was on probation after serving a six-month sentence in a maximum-security federal prison in Wyoming for Schedule I drug possession, and he had gotten tired of meeting with his probation officer. Unfortunately, without telling his PO or anyone else, he packed his few belongings, left town, and began a new life on the West Coast. More unfortunately, he either forgot to change his name first or figured he'd never be found.

One day, a few months after Eddie moved in, he called me from work to let me know he would not be home to feed Sadie dinner. He said he had just been arrested by two federal probation officers who had walked into the tour boat office and asked for him by name. He was being escorted at that moment to Sea-Tac airport and was being flown straight back to Wyoming. He said he was very sorry. He sounded sorry. I guess I was Eddie's "one phone call." He was not allowed to come back to the condo to change clothes, pack a bag, eat a snack, or pat Sadie good-bye. Thankfully, Eddie's boss was understanding and came to pick up his belongings the following week, carrying them away in four or five large black plastic garbage bags. Eddie explained everything in a letter a few weeks later.

I was a bit surprised and a little stunned, but I regrouped quickly. *Okay*, I thought, *I guess it's time to start checking references. I probably should have done that with my husband.*

A couple of tenants later, in the fall of 2009, came Rafe. He was lively, lovely, and hilariously funny, and in his early thirties; he was tall and round and resembled a more handsome version of the Pillsbury Doughboy, with a pleasant paunch and a buzz cut of dark brown hair.

He found me on Craigslist too. Or maybe I found him. By now, I had learned to ask for work and tenant references, as well as proof of financial ability to pay. Rafe had moved to Seattle from Portland, Oregon, to fulfill a childhood dream of becoming a Seattle Metro bus driver—he loved anything that had an engine and chugged. He had a sweetheart named Arnie, who was still living in Portland, was a few years younger than Rafe, and was similarly lovely and a bit shy. Once Rafe moved in, he and Arnie visited each other back and forth on alternate weekends. This worked out fine; they were courteous, quiet, thoughtful, and amiable when they were here together, and they were so good to each other. I became fond of both of them.

Rafe was indeed a lovely tenant, but just one itty-bitty thing wasn't quite right. He arrived with the most aggressive feline companion I have ever known when it came to getting along with other cats. I do not exaggerate. She was a four-year-old, rotund, slate-gray, short-haired bundle of boundless energy. Her name was Sugar. She would have been more aptly named Hot Pepper in her cat-stalking moments. On the day she and Rafe moved in, Sugar greeted me with a nonchalant leg rub and then proceeded within the first hour to try to murder Sadie. Somehow, Sadie had sneaked into Rafe's room unseen during the hubbub of unpacking and setting up and was obliviously sniffing around in the corners. Sugar spotted her and was poised to pounce. I saw this and could tell Sugar was not going to let Sadie escape with any of her nine lives to spare. I dove and scooped Sadie up in the nick of time. We all agreed right then that it would be best for Sugar to spend her "leisure time" (which was all the time—I guess domesticated cats don't have "nonleisure time") in Rafe's room with the door closed.

Everyone was pleased with that arrangement, including Sugar. She was happy being the "grande dame" of the big bedroom suite with its long, wide window ledge, from where she would tuck her paws underneath her gray belly and sit like a sphinx so she could monitor the birds and the weather. And Sadie calmly maintained her alpha-cat reign over the rest of the place. Rafe and Sugar lived with me for about two years, until Arnie was able to transfer to Seattle. Sugar and the boys eventually found a nice apartment in Bellevue and moved there, and Rafe and Arnie got married about a year later. That was a just-right-to-almost-perfect tenant match. I still talk with Rafe occasionally and follow him and Arnie on Facebook. Sadly, Sugar eventually met her maker, but the guys have remained dedicated pet parents and have adopted more cat children over the years.

Time passed, life went on, and more tenants came and went. An eager, young vegan couple in their early twenties, Lizzy and Raul, moved in with their sweet, mellow, three-year-old hound dog named Posie. She sported gray and brown spots, was low to the ground, and had weak back legs, so she mostly scooted around on her bottom in the house, but she was pain-free, placid, and uncomplaining. She had a big, goofy, slobbery-lipped grin and the friendliest, round, gray Betty Boop eyes. She won my heart the minute those eyes caught mine.

Her owners—I called them "the kids"—came laden with super-sized, black-plastic garbage bags filled with cartons of rice and grains, boxes of sugar-free buckwheat cereal and gluten-free pasta, and packages of spicy curry paste, smoothie mixes, and wild-caught skipjack tuna. They brought paper grocery bags brimming with feathery star-shaped fronds of wild fennel, bulbous beets, green onions, leafy lettuces, and other veggies and fruits. They brought kitchen implements and accessories, including two blenders, an air fryer, a rice cooker, a Wolfgang Puck indoor reversible electric grill and griddle, pots and pans and mixing bowls, a couple of rolling pins, and a dozen wooden spoons and assorted spatulas. They also brought a full-size futon mattress and other supersize plastic garbage bags—these were white—filled with clothes, bedding, and a set of floor-to-ceiling tie-dyed curtains in vivid blues, oranges, and pinks they had made themselves. They hung the curtains right away, and the room was transformed into a cheerful, young hippie hangout. It was a bit tight squeezing all their kitchen foodstuffs and sundries into their half of the fridge and on their designated counter space. But I was optimistic. *They certainly are health-conscious*, I thought. *And eager.*

Their first night here, Lizzie and Raul were exhausted and fell asleep early with their bedroom door closed, as was the proper tenant etiquette, but left Posie the hound dog, apparently forgotten but peacefully asleep, on the rug in the foyer hallway. I am sure she was exhausted too. I guess they hadn't walked her before bed—or not enough—

because during the night, she pooped abundant but tidy and perfectly formed miniature Tootsie Rolls of doggie doo on the rug. These sweet Tootsies didn't even stink, and there was no mess to deal with when the kids hurriedly scooped them up early the next morning. They expressed remorse. But the next day, Lizzie overstuffed the clothes washer with too many towels and a couple of fluffy blankets, and it overflowed. They expressed more remorse. A few days after that, they had a disconcertingly raucous argument that sounded like it was edging perilously close to physical blows, but it didn't. It scared me, though. This time, they did not express remorse. Other things happened, too. They lasted one month. I had to let them go. I didn't miss them, but I missed Posie, the sweet, goofy-grinned hound dog and her adoring, gray Betty Boop eyes.

So, yes, the good-tenant trajectory was skidding downhill fast and was just about to hit a rocky bottom. I was doing the best I could and trying to understand how to make this tenant thing work. As I contemplated, one thing was clear: I was always trying to be nice, feeling guilty if I tried to set firm limits, and thinking that if someone balked and became uncooperative, I had to be the one to fix the situation and I needed to wait until it became unbearable to take action. It was now the beginning of summer 2020, and the Covid pandemic had begun in earnest. By this time, finding someone willing and able to abide by strict Covid precautions was vital. Continuing my Craigslist search for the next compatible tenant prospect, I found Lane. I reached out, we chatted on the phone, and then we met in person. We talked on the phone again once or twice, and he seemed amiable and cooperative, a regular guy. He was a bit quiet and shy, but again, there was nothing wrong with that, and his references checked out. And he was interested. So, I asked him to move in. He liked to cook and promised to teach me how to bake lemon scones.

Lane was an almost-divorced IT specialist in his early forties, who arrived with his massively muscled, sleek, smoky gray and black–striped, green-eyed male cat Hernando. You may have realized by now that I am a pushover for goo-goo-eyed cats—and the occasional dog. Hernando was one such cat. What could go wrong? On the first day, this sweet thing sidled up to me, purring like a small motorboat, gently caressing my legs with his body, saying, "May I rub against you, please, Rosie?

Will you be my friend?" That gesture was just like Sugar's, but without the violent streak.

Hernando ignored Sadie from the start, but he soon commandeered her favorite sunlit spot on the living room rug in front of the wide, floor-to-ceiling glass sliding doors that led to the deck and the bird action. He would sit for hours, silent and unmoving as a rock except for his slowly blinking eyes and twitching nose, whiskers, and tail, and an occasional high-pitched "eee-eee-ee—I see you, birdies!" as he stared out at the black-capped chickadees, red-breasted nuthatches, ruby-throated hummingbirds, and other amiable avian visitors. It was clear that Hernando considered these critters potentially tender, mouthwatering, cat-snackable morsels, but fortunately, the locked sliding doors made this a nonissue.

Occasionally, if I was on the living room couch, reading, eating, journaling, or folding laundry while I watched PBS on the big-screen TV, Hernando would abandon his watch and climb up into my lap, blink up at me with his big, sexy honeydew-green eyes, make a couple of graceful full circles with his body, ooze down, and doze off, head nuzzled against my chest. Sadie seemed fine with that arrangement and was not jealous. She knew she was top cat. She would take up her post in her second favorite avian viewing area on the wide window ledge in our bedroom. She continued to roam at will throughout the condo unit, and she and Hernando lived in seemingly blissful but purposeful ignorance of each other. I was fine with that arrangement, too. Hernando was a sweetheart. Have I mentioned his big, sexy, slow-blinking green eyes?

Lane, however, was another matter. He was good-looking and slightly stoop-shouldered at six feet plus, with a wide frame, a pale complexion, and a shock of short, thick, curly white-blond hair. In the beginning, he was, as I had anticipated, low-key, cooperative, and quiet. He slept on a single-bed-size mattress on the floor in a corner of his room and didn't have much more than that. "It was the result of the divorce," he explained. "I didn't get to keep anything." As it turned out, Lane was deeply depressed (*who wouldn't be after a divorce like that?*). He slept in a lot, took sick days often, and—I soon realized—drank secretly alone in his room late at night. I, of course, did not allow excessive alcohol use. Lane scolded Hernando mercilessly and often for "meowing too loud and bothering Rosie." When I assured Lane that it was not a problem and that Hernando was just being a cat, Lane insisted that Hernando "understood what to do and not do" and was just being a "brat!" Uh…okay.

Within the first ten days or so, I began to hear Lane mumbling obscenities late at night behind the closed door of his room, very low and drunkenly, but menacing and loud enough for me to hear him from the kitchen, where I was often puttering at that time of the evening. But hey, he was a decent guy, and I was a nice person. I felt bad for him. I gave him a couple of chances to either stop drinking or go to AA or counseling, and he promised he would but did none of those things. His late-night behavior continued. Finally, three months later, after further unsuccessful negotiations, I evicted him. When Lane moved out, I heaved a great sigh of relief. I'm sure he did, too. We were not sorry to say goodbye to each other, but—you guessed it—I was sad to say goodbye to the dashing and handsome Hernando.

It is also important to note, with blindingly bright hindsight, that, although I didn't think of them as such at the time, all these tenant departures—from the fond, tearful ones to the "thank God, that's over" ones—triggered real grief, and they took their toll. They were clear instances of disenfranchised grief, including—and in some cases, *especially*—the departures of the pets, whom I mostly loved and adored (except for Sugar, of course…well, maybe even her, a little) *because* I did not think of those experiences in that way. To me, they were life lessons learned, friends made, lost, and bid adieu bittersweet and otherwise, but *not* as grief, and certainly not grief with a capital G.

Lane was my rock bottom, the last straw, and the end of the road. Um…did I mention I was done? So, I took a few weeks off from searching for someone new and sat myself down for a serious, soul-searching conversation. This condo was my home and my haven. I needed to feel comfortable and safe. I needed to take more time evaluating prospective clients and asking more questions. And I needed to reestablish and recommit to my top requirements for a successful landlord-tenant experience, as well as to healthy landlady-tenant boundaries I needed to maintain once someone moved in! Okay, so just what were these requirements and boundaries? I knew them. I just needed to articulate them and then write them down.

The result was my Top Five Must-Have Qualifications List for the Essential Roomie. (With affectionate apologies to Coleman Barks's 1995 book titled *The Essential Rumi* [pronounced room-ee], a compilation of translated poetry and writings by the famous thirteenth-century Islamic Sufi poet, mystic, and scholar Jalal A-al-Din Muhammad Rumi, popularly known in modern times simply as Rumi.) And to my longtime Seattle friend, Ami, whom you will meet again later in this book—and who was as enamored with Rumi as I was.

Here's how that happened. I had bought the dusty, red leather–bound book one day at a thrift store and it was on my bookshelf at home. During one of our occasional long-distance phone calls, Ami and I were discussing the book; at that moment, she, who was well acquainted with my long and storied roommate history, burst forth spontaneously with the play on words that sparked the idea: "Hey, Rosie! You're a good writer! You could write a book called *The Essential Roomie*! Get it?"

We giggled. Ever since that day, she had teased me about writing that book in whose pages I would captivate readers with that housemate history. It was true, I loved to write, and writing a book was a fun dream. But, I didn't think I had a book in me, especially one about my adventures with a bunch of wild and crazy housemates. Alas, that was before Kevin.

Rosie's Top Five Must-Have Qualifications List for the Essential Roomie
Renters must follow these rules within reason:
1. Be kind;
2. Communicate well around household issues;
3. Keep one's personal and especially common areas reasonably clean;
4. Be at least minimally self-aware and self-reflective about
    a. Their own emotional needs; and
    b. Their pet's needs and capacities to "understand";
5. Have a mostly drama-free life, maybe a few good friends, and a few personal and professional interests and goals.

This may seem like a daunting list, but I thought these five must-haves were all within reason. It was also important, of course, that ideal roomies would share my common political, LGBTQIA+ friendly, and other social justice values. These political compatibilities were not listed in the top five since they were givens for me and nonnegotiable. In my defense, I had stayed mostly true to those nonnegotiables by always describing them in excruciating detail in my "seeking tenant" Craigslist ads.

It turned out that making this list, checking it more than twice, and my humble recommitment to good boundary-keeping seemed to work, because that's when Kevin arrived.

Thanks again, dearest Ami. And, you too, Rumi.

CHAPTER FOUR

Life with Kevin—
the Calm Before the Storm

AT SIX O'CLOCK on Sunday evening, October 18, 2020, at the height of the Covid pandemic, Kevin Boggs came to interview with me and Sadie about moving into the primary bedroom suite. I found him on Craigslist. Well, yes, it was still Craigslist, and I was wary, but I had updated my long, detailed profile, I had my wits about me, and I had my top-five list memorized. Kevin and I had talked on the phone twice earlier in the week. He had an easy laugh and a kind voice, and he answered questions candidly. I had checked his personal and work references. They were filled with praise and stable financial numbers. And he was the father of a tuxedo cat named Jasmine.

I had a copy of The List in my pocket when Kevin arrived, just in case I got nervous and forgot what it said. The first things I noticed were his kind, twinkling green eyes and then his gentle voice and easy laugh—the same as on the phone. All this, despite the medical mask he was wearing in deference to my Covid protocol rules. I showed him around the place and the room that would be his. He asked questions and nodded and smiled. Then we sat down at my little round dining room table to talk. Our conversation lasted about two and a half hours. The talk was deep and genuine and mutual. We laughed and chuckled, and the eye contact was good. When he talked lovingly about Jasmine, my heart went pitter-patter.

When we stopped talking, there was a comfortable silence. Then Kevin said something like, "Rosie, this place is incredible…and you… you are amazing, and Jasmine and I would really like to live here with you and Sadie. What can I say to make you choose us? I can pay more rent than you're asking if that'll help make a difference!" I had had a couple of other people come see the place, but no one with whom I was enamored. I blushed and checked in with my "gut," which I had started to call my "divine inner goddess intuition." My gut-goddess was smiling. Kevin had checked off all five boxes on the Top Five Must-Have Qualifications List for the Essential Roomie and more. He seemed kind and in no way crazy. And, there was Jasmine. I looked at him and said, "Okay…I choose you guys." We laughed some more. Kevin returned the following Sunday, October 25, and we signed the lease.

On November 1, he arrived with Jasmine in her large blue carrier. She was big, fluffy, black and mostly white, furry, and plump, a purring ball of eagerness and amiability. Kevin opened the door of the carrier, and Jasmine sniffed her way out into the room. Kevin gently lifted Jasmine up in his big arms, exuding tenderness. As the days went by, I would see him swoop her up and hold her in the air close to his face and look into her big, gold cat eyes as she gazed down into his. Often her pupils would relax into sleepy black slits, and she would put a front paw up and delicately touch Kevin's nose.

When Kevin moved in, he was just shy of his forty-seventh birthday. He was tall, gangly, and broad-shouldered, and he carried himself with a shy, awkward eagerness. He had a smooth, ivory complexion, a smooth-shaven head, and that wide, impish smile. His features were handsomely chiseled, and his profile sometimes reminded me of the Greek statue of Adonis or Michelangelo's *David*.

He had been a talented glass artist and woodworker and more recently had been through some seriously hardscrabble times, including drug addiction and a brief stay in a homeless camp community. We talked about all that during our two-hour-plus chat. But, for the past five years, he had been on a solid road to recovery. Now, a vital piece of his daily life was counseling other people who were struggling to free themselves from similar dire circumstances. He wrote to me in an email before moving in, "My time there [in the homeless community] is what motivated me to become an advocate for the homeless and then a recovery coach."

Kevin had been working these five years as a Navy ship welder at a well-respected shipyard on Harbor Island near the West Seattle Bridge.

He was content and had life goals. He had his continuing, stable recovery and had made amends and reconciled with his parents, who loved him with every fiber of their beings. He had a few close, trusted friends and satisfying work with an excellent salary. He looked forward to returning to his art someday. He was a devoted father to Jasmine. And he had been looking for a safe haven. And now he felt he had found it. He and Jasmine were here with me.

Sweet Jasmine adored Sadie at first sight. Sadly, Sadie did not reciprocate Jasmine's affections. Sadie was fifteen years old now, still petite, active, and set in her alpha-cat ways. Jasmine was not deterred. She was enraptured. She followed Sadie everywhere, so Kevin and I would supervise these close encounters with care. That's partly how our bonding began. We would take up our supervision stations and hang out in the living room, as we watched Jasmine skitter and creep around behind Sadie, who would often be walking regally through the room, seemingly unaware of Jasmine's presence. Sometimes Jasmine would get close enough to hop as delicately as a grasshopper onto Sadie's tail; Jasmine, unfortunately, weighed a bit more than a grasshopper, and Sadie, having none of it, would whirl around, puff up and growl or hiss and swat at Jasmine; Jasmine would go down on her back like a dead thing, but playfully, her paws up in the air, as if silently pleading for mercy. Kevin and I made sure there was no bloodshed, but they never got close to that. We'd whoop and laugh and scoop them up and hug them and tell them what good kitties they were. "What a good visit," we'd say to each other with a fist-bump version of a high five. It was Covid, after all. No touching allowed.

Kevin worked the swing shift six days a week, and occasionally on Sundays, at the shipyard. I began to look forward to his one day off, when he would hang out at home, doing laundry, cooking, and Zooming with his parents in front of his laptop at the kitchen counter. We'd cross paths off and on, chat, and have bonding sessions with the cats. I just liked having him around. It was easy, comfortable, and comforting. On the occasional weekends when he had both days off, it felt to me like I was getting a special treat. We had similar schedules that allowed us to sleep in, and we'd often end up silently offering each other a good-morning wave or nod or grunt—*I like you, but don't talk to me yet*—at around noon.

At night, Kevin would usually arrive home from the shipyard at 11:35 p.m., give or take a few minutes, just when Stephen Colbert began his nightly monologue on *The Late Show* on CBS. I'd be on the couch watching the show, while Kevin would stand at his place at the kitchen island and watch along with me while he ate—inhaled, really—one of his mega-burritos that he'd picked up from some late-night-takeout dive on the way home. These monster burritos contained about a million grams of fat and salt. When I expressed concern, he didn't mind. But he wasn't worried, he said. His blood pressure was fine, and he saw his doctor regularly.

"So don't worry, Rosie," he'd tease. "I'm not gonna die on you."

He'd stand there scarfing down those burritos, and we'd shriek with laughter, righteous outrage, and sometimes a few tears, at Colbert's hilarious and terrifying words on the TV screen, and we'd commiserate about the eventual hoped-for end of the MAGA Republican administration of our dear demented, orange-haired president. Sometimes Kevin would share hair-raising, politically incorrect comments made by some of his workmates, and we'd shriek and moan and laugh even more.

Kevin's Sunday morning routine was cooking up massive, steaming-hot batches of organic rolled oats in a big pot on the glass-top stove and then separating them into six sixteen-ounce servings by pouring them into six hard-plastic containers with matching blue lids and storing them in the freezer for the coming week's breakfasts. Afterward, he would clean up the kitchen meticulously without scratching the stovetop, humming to himself as he wiped down any splatters and burnt oatmeal bits left on the glass.

There were so many endearing things about Kevin—his amiable, easy, good-humored presence; his spontaneous laugh; his gentle way with Jasmine and Sadie; and his willingness to do all things helpful around the house, like replacing lightbulbs, building a secure cat door, or vacuuming the living room. He turned me on to the greatest carpet-spot-remover spray in the world. He'd accompany me to Goodwill at the drop of a hat to look for flannel shirts or cute mugs. I appreciated the way he talked so lovingly about his parents and his unflagging adoration of Jasmine. He was such a good sport when I consistently beat him at Scrabble, despite his always putting up a valiant fight.

"Damn, Rosie, you beat me again!" He'd roll his eyes and grin. And we would talk.

At this point, you might reasonably wonder if I had fallen in love with Kevin. The answer is no. It was not like that. I was seventy-one years old, and Kevin was forty-six, albeit almost forty-seven. Indeed, I have always liked younger men (maybe that was part of what the "man problem" was all about!), but that would have been a little too much "cougar," even for me. Anyway, that's not how I felt. Instead, I felt a warm, fuzzy, companionship-style comfort blossoming, blooming, and expanding in my heart. And I would think, *Wow, Rosie, that lonely, yearning feeling you always carry around...of being without a sweetheart? Well, I'm kinda not feeling it these days! Jeeze, so maybe if I never find my sweetheart, as long as Kevin's living here, I'll be fine.* And I was. I don't know why. Maybe Kevin and I had known each other in a past life. So, no, I did not fall in love with him. But I soon came to love him. He became my soul friend, my platonic soul companion. I was simply not aware of how deeply I loved him until he was gone. And, not even then, at first. But, acknowledging the depth of that love would mean acknowledging the depth of the grief I had over the loss of him—genuine, valid, deep grief.

Soon after Kevin moved in, I found myself jokingly saying to him once a week or so as we stood in the kitchen preparing lunch or dinner at our respective countertops, "Hey, Kevin, have I told you lately how happy I am that you're living here?" I wanted to make sure he knew.

After a few more weeks, it was "And oh, by the way, you really should think about living here for the rest of your life!" I was pretty sure he did know by then how genuinely grateful I was to have him and Jasmine living in my home with me and Sadie.

After a few more weeks, I was no longer goofing around. I'd say, "You know, I've decided you *have* to live here forever, okay?" and I'd grin at him. Kevin would guffaw shyly, with just a hint of a nod, and lower his eyes, but I could see his smile, and I knew he was pleased. I was pleased too. He would stay forever. We had a deal.

CHAPTER FIVE

Life After Kevin—
Disenfranchised Grief Comes to Call

KEVIN KEPT HIS PROMISE to live with me forever. He stayed until his "forever" arrived on Sunday, June 6, 2021, seven months and six days after he moved in.

This is what happened. On April 8, 2021, Kevin signed a one-year lease renewal that would begin on May 1. Toward the end of May, he paid June's rent a few days early. All was well.

On Saturday evening, May 29, of Memorial Day weekend, after a couple of hours of heated but friendly competition, I trounced Kevin in Scrabble as usual. He was an especially gracious loser that night. Maybe because he had a three-day weekend off from work. Or maybe because he had spent a few hours the previous Saturday night patiently guiding me through the basics of chess; Kevin was an excellent chess player, and chess was a game that I had never attempted, nor had I ever thought about attempting. And it was a game, we both saw at once, at which I would never beat him (though in my dreams, I would have loved to!). At the end of the evening's several long practice games, I said, "Thanks, Kevin…I know I'll never get these last few hours back, but now I know what chess is all about, and I'm glad to say I'll never have to play it again!" We cracked up and did our Covid fist-bump across the table. Then we said goodnight.

We were both planning to hang around the house over the holiday weekend, completing our respective housecleaning tasks, doing laundry, and avoiding the holiday madding crowds. Maybe we would catch each other coming and going and have a conversation in passing, or drop by

Goodwill. Maybe we'd order out dinner from Persepolis Persian Grill in the University District. They were open for takeout during Covid; the food was incredible, and the hole-in-the-wall place had become a favorite of ours. Or, I might beat him at Scrabble again.

On Sunday morning, I was up and having breakfast at around eleven when Kevin appeared in the doorway of his bedroom dressed in a T-shirt and an old pair of running shorts, just long enough to tell me he had a fever, felt awful, and was going back to bed. He looked awful, too, and his skin was pale and pasty, not like his normal glowing alabaster. We exchanged looks of dour commiseration. He turned around and slumped back into his room, closing the door gently behind him. I was sad for him and disappointed. There would be no fun-filled holiday Sunday and Monday with more low-key, good-natured hang-out time. *Well, maybe next weekend*, I consoled myself. I could not know then that there would not be another of those weekends. Because, by the following Sunday, Kevin would be dead.

***

I promise to tell you how Kevin died, but first I want to share what happened to me during those first chaotic weeks after his death. It's important to paint the picture of just how bad things got and how I came to know about disenfranchised grief.

During those first weeks after Kevin died, I cried, mostly at night in bed, but there was no relief in it. A sense of shock and stunning disbelief took hold of me and hung in the too-heavy air around me. How could this have happened? Where did he go? And why? I felt mostly numb, but my chest and belly hurt constantly. The ache was not pain exactly, but a gnawing, anxious pressure in my chest moving down into my stomach, and it was crushing the breath out of me. I knew it wasn't a heart attack. I knew it was sadness, how big a sadness I could not grasp, but I knew it was too big—too big to believe and too big to handle. At times, I felt as if I were wandering around somewhere outside my body, behind that foggy screen people describe, looking in at that person who was me and feeling that weight bearing down on me.

After the initial shock began to wear off, I started to feel new, terrible sensations in my body. This was a tough transition. My body was racked with blatant, unvarnished despair. I began to cry on and off all day, every day. I still felt queasy and sick to my stomach, a hard knot of grief having settled there, and my interest in food was missing in action. At night, I'd sob quietly into my pillow, wrecked by the deafening quiet of the place until I'd eventually fall asleep from sheer exhaustion.

Within a few weeks of Kevin's death, the voice of my *inner critic* showed up, right on schedule. I wasn't aware of this impending arrival ahead of time, but apparently, my inner critic was and did. It shrieked at me: "You were just Kevin's landlady! Why are *you* feeling so wretched? This deep grief does not belong to you. It belongs to his parents, his brothers, their families, and his longtime friend and fellow welder Caitlin. This is *their* grief. You were not his girlfriend or his wife; you didn't even know him that long. Sure, he was a nice guy, and you loved having him and his cat around the house."

My closest girlfriends seemed to understand my devastation at first—"It was so sudden, after all, and he was so nice," they said. But after those first few weeks, even they began to hint that they wanted me to "start feeling better." They were worried about me, and they were trying to help. Their sentiments were well-intentioned. But these good intentions did not help—they only made me feel guiltier.

My inner critic kept up its nagging harangue. Eventually, after I became familiar with the concept of disenfranchised grief, I designated her a female. She became Blanche. You might know Blanche DuBois, the lonely and beautiful porcelain-skinned protagonist of Tennessee Williams's 1947 Pulitzer Prize-winning play *A Streetcar Named Desire*, who must always "depend upon the kindness of strangers," since no one she knew took seriously her mental anguish, shame, and grief. I thought the name was appropriate.

Blanche knew me to my core; she knew where to strike, and she had good aim—and she was so damn loud. "Come on, Rosie, this is not your grief," she'd admonish. "Your grief is just not that bad, and no one is going to continue to support you, so get over it, already. Here's what you need to do with your feelings—go do something else, go binge-watch some Netflix, have a box of Milk Duds or a pint of Rocky Road ice cream, or a quart, eat till you're sick, or don't eat at all…or go to bed for a day or two or longer, and don't even *think* about taking walks or meditating or doing yoga in your bedroom late at night, or anything else remotely related to 'self-care.' Whatever you do, do *not* grieve in front of anyone—your friends, strangers—at work or in public places. Do not grieve alone in bed or in the shower. Even better, simply don't grieve at all. Shut it down, girl, shut it all down!"

I tried not to listen, but Blanche was persistent. Her voice was the old, deeply ingrained inner chastiser I knew so intimately; it was the voice of self-judgment and shame. That voice was disenfranchising my grief over Kevin and my right to claim it as mine. That voice wanted me to grieve quickly and get over it. I was ashamed that I could not obey.

Nevertheless, I did my best. One evening, I was writing in one of my journals in response to an online grief prompt that asked, "If your grief could speak to you, what would it say?" I had been writing to these prompts for a few weeks, and it seemed to help clarify things, as writing often does for me. Okay, I was grieving, and I was determined to "do it right." So, I wrote. And hot tears welled up. I kept grabbing Kleenex. *Okay, this might be good,* I thought—at least I hoped so. *Maybe something important will come out of this. Maybe I'll finally get some relief.*

And something did come. What came was a voice that said, *Thank you, Rosie. I am here. I am your grief; it's about time. I'm feeling so left out. Please pay attention to me. Please hold me and care for me. And tell Blanche to shut up and go for a walk herself.* Ah, I thought and kept scribbling. The message was becoming clear: *Please don't shame me, don't ignore me, don't belittle me. I am simply sadness, devastating sadness. Kevin was your friend, your heart family, and you loved him, no matter how short a time you knew him. You still do love him, and you miss him fiercely. That is okay. That is normal. You are allowed to claim that love forever, and to claim me—your grief—as your own.*

In that moment, as I looked at the words I had scrawled, I understood with a sudden clarity and some amazement (plus subtle but significant doses of humility, relief, and gratitude), that I had been discounting—and shaming—this fierce grief I was feeling over Kevin's death. Ah, the shame.

It was not quite that quick a fix, unfortunately. I wasn't instantly transformed. My grief still felt "not quite okay." The shame was especially hard to resist.

Fortunately, just days later, while scrolling through the now ubiquitous grief articles online (it was still Covid times, after all), I stumbled across Dr. Ken Doka and the concept of disenfranchised grief.[3] That was the eureka moment I spoke of earlier. And in that moment, I finally understood that the enormity of the grief I felt was okay. My grief *was* bad enough. And I began to take the first wobbly, unpredictable baby steps along the path of my true grief-healing journey. I began to understand that the shame part of my grief and my self-belittling self-torment was nothing other than being drowned in what was called "disenfranchised grief." It had a name! And I began to learn what was at risk by keeping my grief hidden, by considering it "not bad enough." I began to learn how to transform it into "grief with a capital G," grief that was as valid as anyone else's and no longer something to be ashamed of, no longer something to hide. It was no longer disenfranchised at all.

By August, with a tiny glint of renewed hope, relief, and optimism mixed with an odd and intricate mix of puzzlement, resentment, and disbelief, I found a lovely new tenant named Hannah (yes, through Craigslist). She had found my ad, in which this time I had restated in painstaking detail all about myself and my "essential roomie qualifications," and she had reached out to me; she was twenty-four years old, moving up to Seattle from Albuquerque—with her cat!—to begin working on her master's degree in social work at the University of Washington. She would not be arriving in Seattle until late September, and I was grateful for the added time to do my private grief work. She would be a good fit.

CHAPTER SIX

The Storm—
How the End Began

I PROMISED I WOULD tell you the story of how Kevin died. Here it is.

My brain wasn't working well enough for me to write in my occasional journal as events unfolded during that week when Kevin was sick. But, somehow I felt it was important to document what was happening. I wanted to remember so Kevin and I could laugh about it later. So, I scribbled a few words each night in the tiny, by-date boxes in my five by seven–inch, spiral-bound appointment book while he lay in bed in his room, sleeping most of the time and spiking a consistently too-high fever of around 104 degrees Fahrenheit.

My 2021 appointment book was like the yearly calendar books I have used forever to write down appointments with clients, adventures with friends and visiting family members, doctor and dentist appointments, dates with potential husbands, etcetera. I'm still too old-fashioned to use the calendar on my iPhone. It's too complicated, the phone will die at some point, and I'll be lost. So I scribbled.

I tried not to bother Kevin the rest of that first Sunday. On Monday, he was no better. When I checked in on him a few times, he asked me if I would feed Jasmine. I said, of course.

I kept sticking my face through his doorway. By Tuesday morning, he was still no better. He had not eaten a thing and was not hungry. I fussed and worried. Around ten o'clock, although he grumbled, he let me coerce him into letting me drive him to a nearby urgent care clinic, and then, on their recommendation, to the emergency room of the University of Washington's Northwest Hospital a few blocks away. His temperature was too high for the walk-in clinic to treat him, and they urged us to follow their advice and go.

The ER kept Kevin for hours. Once they finally had an examining room ready for him, he lay disconsolate on a bed, clad in a long blue and white–striped hospital gown. The room was stark and sterile-looking—we had not expected the Ritz—while he was given all kinds of tests, including Covid, urine tests, and a million blood tests. His vital signs were taken constantly, and he was hydrated through an IV since he couldn't keep food down. He muttered and complained the whole time to whoever was there about wanting to go home, and none of the tests had turned up anything by around midnight that night, except that he did not have Covid. He told me all this in grudging, graphic detail later on during the drive home.

When Kevin was first taken back into the examining room, I hung around in the waiting area among a dozen or so other miserable-looking sick people and their companions. After about a half hour, I checked with the reception desk to see if they had any updates. I kept checking and kept checking, and they kept telling me, "It'll probably be a while." I found lunch—a bag of mixed nuts, a chocolate bar, and a bottle of water—from one of the hospital's vending machines and ate outside, sitting at a comfy, wrought-iron patio table in a small tree-lined eating area near the ER entrance. It was relaxing. The sky was a brilliant, cloudless blue, and the sun was hot, but the temperature was caressingly and breezily mild. It was a typical glorious Seattle summer day without a hint of humidity in the air. I was relieved that Kevin was being looked after and that everything would be fine. It would be fun to tell him all this later once he felt better.

After I ate, I checked in again with the receptionist. She made another call to the back and told me that it would still be a while. She added that it would be all right for me to go home if I wanted to, and that someone would call me when I needed to come back to take Kevin home. It was about two by then. I went home.

I called to check in periodically throughout the rest of the day, and it wasn't until about nine that night that I was told Kevin would probably be released within the next hour or two, and that I was welcome to come back any time. I could not think of one more thing to do at home, so I drove back.

At the hospital, I was ushered back to the examining room where Kevin was still lying in bed, dressed in the same hospital gown and still hooked up to IVs. The emergency room doctor, a young, thin guy in blue scrubs with a mass of curly black hair and a bushy, well-groomed beard, was talking with Kevin about what to do once he was discharged. The doctor said it was extremely important for him to continue to take Tylenol and keep drinking water. I stood watching this scene unfold and thought, *Something is not right with this picture.* Here was my very grumpy, six-foot-four tenant, chafing to be out of there but still looking horribly pale and still with the 104-degree fever he'd had for three days, and who hadn't been able to keep food down, sometimes not even water.

I raised my eyebrows at Kevin, but I don't think he saw me, and if he did, he did not pay attention. "I just wanna go home," he kept muttering. The ER doctor said he could. So, who was I to argue with the ER doctor, much less with Kevin? I stepped out while he got dressed; then we gathered his things, Kevin picked up his discharge papers at the front desk, and we slowly made our way to my car. He didn't lean on me, although I offered. He lumbered along, looking like an exhausted old man. He was shivering as he folded his long body into the front passenger seat of my car. He buckled himself in, and I got in on the driver's side and drove us home. In a disdainful, exhausted tone, Kevin regaled me about the endless, torturous tests and bodily invasions he had endured, repeating again and again, "All this time wasted for nothing…ridiculous." I did not argue.

***

That night and through the next day, Kevin slept and slept. I quietly opened his door a crack every once in a while to peek in. He looked about the same—pasty white and a bit restless and sometimes with a grimace on his lips, but mercifully asleep. Every few hours, I'd wake him and give him a couple of Tylenol with water, which he was able to swallow, and I'd take his temperature. It was always the same—still 104.

That was the day that Kevin and I had "the conversation" about what to do if he wasn't feeling better in another day or two. I'd call

Caitlin and tell her what was going on, and maybe have her—or someone—come hang out with him for a couple of hours, so I could get some errands done. (Ironically, the private eldercare client I had at the moment was spending a month in a rehab facility some distance away, so I was home with nothing else to do but listen for noises through the door of Kevin's bedroom and try to distract myself with things like attending to Sadie and my own life.) He said okay. I fed Jasmine, scratched her ears, cleaned her litter box, and told her everything would be okay.

By Wednesday night around ten o'clock, I cracked Kevin's bedroom door open for the umpteenth time and looked in. He was awake. He gave me a weak smile. He had drunk only water over these last few days, but he still did not feel like eating and didn't want to try. "I'm not hungry anyway, and I'll probably just throw up again if I try to eat," he said, his smile turning wry at my offer to fix him something simple like toast.

Then he let me take his temperature again. I was using my vintage thermometer, circa 1974, with real liquid mercury inside its clear plastic casing that always recorded temperatures accurately. After making sure he kept it under his tongue for at least three minutes, I looked at it, and it read 94.5 degrees Fahrenheit. This did not seem like a good thing to me. I felt his forehead. I can't remember if it was cool or hot, dry or sweaty. Nor do I remember if I asked him how he felt. I do remember that my heart started pounding and my palms started sweating. This could not be good.

"Okay, hang on," I said. "I'm gonna go look this up." I left him briefly, went and sat down in the living room with my iPhone, and Googled "human body temperatures of 94.5." Google read, "If your temperature is near or dipping below 95 degrees, it's too low, and it in-dicates hypothermia. People…can lose consciousness or go into shock… call 911." That was good enough for me. So I called. Then I went back into Kevin's room and told him that Google said his temp indicated hypothermia and the medics were on the way. He grunted, but he did not argue. I had no idea what the medics would find, of course, or what they would do, but I wasn't taking any chances. I wanted them there.

The medics arrived within minutes, four men as big and broad as oak trees, and I led them into Kevin's room, explaining the situation as we went, although they already knew the details from my phone call. They bustled about, taking his temperature and checking the rest of his vital signs. They told us he seemed okay. His temperature, according to their snazzy digital thermometer, was around 97. They politely poo-pooed my insistence on the accuracy of my vintage thermometer and said they were doubtful Kevin's temperature had been 94.5. I knew they were wrong, but who was I to argue with these four massive, strapping, out-of-this-world-gorgeous medics dressed in midnight blue? They were as smart as doctors, right? The important thing was that, according to them, Kevin was stable and should be fine at home. If anything changed, I could feel free to call again. Then they left.

Kevin and I rolled our eyes a little at each other. I wished him a good sleep and left him. In my room, I might have cried a little, I don't remember, but my stomach felt like it had a pile of scorched rocks roiling around inside it. I scribbled a couple of lines about the day in my appointment book and eventually fell asleep.

When my phone rang Thursday morning at around nine, it woke me, and I jumped. It was much too early for my night-owl lifestyle, but I was surprised and grateful that I had slept at all. It was Kevin's dad, George, on the phone. He asked how Kevin was feeling. I'd been on the phone with George and Kevin's mom, Ann, who lived in Southern California, for the past couple of days, briefly updating them on how he was doing. Kevin had told me I could talk to them because he was just too sick to call them himself. Since then, I'd left my phone on in case they called me. I got my slippers on, padded to his room, and knocked softly on his door. I did not hear anything, so I opened the door and went in.

Kevin was leaning against the wall in the doorway between his bathroom and the huge walk-in closet. He was trying to get dressed, and he already had on one of his red-and-black-striped flannel shirts and a pair of jeans. His body was shaking, and his hands were trembling as he finished zipping up his jeans. He glanced at me, and his eyes looked as scared as those deer in the headlights that people talk about.

"The hospital just called and said I have an infection in my blood," he said, his voice barely above a whisper, "and I need to go back to the hospital right away."

I stared at Kevin. I was having my own deer-in-the-headlights moment computing this news. It felt a bit like watching a catastrophic emergency announcement on TV, with too much information flashing across the bottom of the screen all at once. I wondered how he had been able to answer his phone—*How in the heck had he had the presence of mind to keep it charged up all this time? And, how had he had a coherent phone conversation with the hospital, and then follow through by getting his clothes on? And why did the person who called not call me in the first place? They knew the condition he was in, and that I was his contact... how could they possibly have thought that he was clear-headed enough to have this phone conversation and then proceed to do as they told him? And they didn't even have him come get me and put me on the phone? How dare they?* These thoughts enraged me. I said none of this to Kevin as I watched him leaning against the closet door. *But thankfully,* I thought, *somehow, he had.* More thoughts tumbled through my brain. *There's no way I can get him in the car and drive him anywhere like this. I'm gonna have to call 911 again.*

"Okay," I said. "Come sit down here," and I patted the bed. "I'm calling the ambulance again." And again, he did not argue. He looked at me docilely, sat down on the bed, and slowly began putting on his shoes and socks.

I don't remember getting back on the phone to tell George what was happening. I must have, because I needed to get off the phone with him and call 911. I only remember that the medics—a different team than the ones who had been there fewer than twelve hours earlier—arrived, again within minutes, rolling a long gurney down the long hallway and into the condo and Kevin's room. They asked me nothing; they knew their mission. The dispatcher had asked me to make sure there were no pets loose in the house who might become agitated, get underfoot, or attack anyone once they entered the unit. This was not a problem. My own Sadie was always long gone under my bed when confronted by commotion, and poor Jasmine, who was not the kind of cat who was in the habit of attacking anyone ever, had today found her way under Kevin's bed and was hunched up against the farthest wall. When I bent down to look, I could tell she had no intention of coming out until the chaos of the large men in their noisy, heavy shoes and the rumbling gurney subsided. The medics helped Kevin stand up and walked him the few steps to the gurney. They hoisted him on it, strapped him in, and were on their way. *My God, he looks so weak.*

Kevin didn't say anything to me as the medics pushed the gurney back out of the bedroom; he didn't look at me or wave or look back for Jasmine. Everything was happening too fast, and I guess we were both in shock. I didn't say anything either, nor did I move to follow him as the medics rolled him down the foyer hall, out of the condo, and back down the hallway to the elevator. I didn't think about following the ambulance to the hospital in my car; I didn't think about telling him, "Bye, you'll be fine," or "hang in there!" or "Jasmine will be fine!" I just stood there and listened until I couldn't hear them anymore. All I could think of was, *Thank God they finally figured out what's wrong with him, and now they'll take care of him, and get him well, and then he'll come home, and everything will be fine again.* I turned, and, after a little coaxing, Jasmine's pink nose appeared out from under the bed. When the rest of her followed, I gently lifted her into my arms and said "Everything's gonna be okay now, sweetheart. Daddy's gonna be home soon." I did not know that was a lie.

Compelled by an urgent need to straighten up Kevin's room so it would be clean and ready for his return, I began picking up his dirty clothes and towels and threw them in his laundry hamper. I tossed out his crumpled Kleenex and the food and juice boxes and energy drinks he had not consumed, and I put the dirty plates, glasses, and plastic bottles in the dishwasher. I shook out his pillows and blankets, stripped the sweaty sheets off the bed, threw them in my laundry hamper, and put fresh sheets on. I put out food and fresh water for Jasmine and cleaned out her litter box for the umpteenth time. I thought she looked dazed and exhausted, like me. I stroked and patted her and scratched behind her ears.

I don't remember much else about that day, except for the phone call I made later in the afternoon to Northwest Hospital, where the ambulance had taken Kevin and where he had spent that first long day and into the night on Tuesday in the emergency room. I was connected right away with a nurse in intensive care…*intensive care? Why is he in intensive care?* My body went cold. For some strange reason—a small miracle, since despite my not being related to him by blood or marriage, my name was still on the paperwork—she was okay sharing information with me about his condition. She explained that he had been admitted to the ICU because of the staph infection that had developed in his blood, and then she said, "We're having trouble stabilizing his organs."

A tight band of pain began spreading across my forehead. This could not be good. Days later, when I looked back at my notes in my appointment book for that night of June 3, 2021, I saw that I had scribbled, *Kevin in ICU—staph infection in blood.* I had drawn a scared, frowning face emoji next to it. The notes in the book also said that I had talked with George, but I don't remember when or what I said. I know it was after the ambulance took Kevin back to the hospital, and it must have been before I talked with the ICU nurse. Yes, that must have been what happened.

CHAPTER SEVEN

No Turning Back

ON FRIDAY MORNING, I paced, and then I called Northwest Hospital again. I was told that Kevin had been transferred. *Transferred! Transferred? What? Why? When?* I could not have heard that right, but I had. This was all too confusing. It was impossible. But the kind woman on the phone explained that he'd been taken to the University of Washington Medical Center's main campus about five miles from Northwest and was admitted to the cardiac intensive care unit. By then, that's what he needed, and Northwest did not have a CICU. I was not relieved. I was terrified.

I thanked her, hung up, and called the main campus number for UWMC that I had quickly jotted down. My hands shook. I explained who I was, and, again, I was connected right away to a physician assistant in the cardiac intensive care unit who was involved with Kevin's care. She introduced herself as Catherine and seemed to also know who I was—another small miracle. I guess my name had made its way into their medical chart by now. She spoke to me in a low, empathetic tone. She said something like, "His chances are not good...you can come see him if you want, but he's hooked up to a lot of tubes, and he's not responding." *Okay*, I thought. *This is not happening.* Although Covid protocols were still in place—families only, and even then, only one at a time—and they knew I was not related, she had said I could come. In fact, she encouraged me. "It's good if you come." Now my whole body was enveloped in waves of nausea. But I knew I would go. I had to. I needed to.

I hung up the phone and dialed George's cell phone number. He picked up right away.

"Rosie, we're still waiting to hear back from Kevin's doctor at UW Medical Center, where they transferred him," George said. "The doctor called us last night, and he said they're watching to see how Kevin responds. He's still really sick, and…if he gets well…it will probably be a long recovery process…so we don't know what's happening yet…the doctor said he'd call again today, but we don't know when." George's voice sounded calm, but I could hear his panicky undertone. "This is all so sudden, Rosie…we just don't know what to do right now, except wait."

My body, already in a cold sweat, turned to ice. I told George what Catherine, the physician's assistant, had said to me minutes earlier.

"George, please," I said. "I don't know what's happening either, but I think you guys should come…so…please come. I just think you should come." I knew I should have been trying to sound calm and reasonable, but I couldn't. I was pleading. I was desperate. I could not do this by myself. And his parents needed to be here. They had to come. For Kevin and for me.

I could hear quiet breathing on the other end of the phone for what felt like a century. Then George said, "Okay, of course…of course…I understand. As soon as we get off the phone, I'll talk to Ann, and we'll make a plane reservation for as soon as possible."

"Oh, thank you, George. Thank you so much, and please try to make it soon," I said.

There was another pause. Then George said, "But, Rosie, I'm thinking…we'll need to rent a car and find a hotel and then get to the hospital somehow…I'm not sure—"

I didn't wait for George to finish his thought. I knew what he was thinking. "No, please, don't worry about any of that, George. You and Ann can stay with me. There's plenty of room, you can sleep in Kevin's room, and I'll drive you to the hospital to see him." Another silence on the other end of the phone. I continued as if it were all decided. "I'll text you the directions to get to my house from the airport, and you can just call a cab or an Uber when you land in Seattle…okay? And George, the nurse said I could go see him tonight, so I'm gonna go, okay?"

"Okay, Rosie, yes, that all sounds perfect," George said, and he sounded relieved. "This is all so kind of you. I'll call you back as soon as we've made reservations, and I'll let you know when we'll be arriving."

I thanked George, and we hung up. My hands shook as I texted him my street address. Relief and sadness surged through me. His parents would come. They would be here for Kevin. They would be here with him. And they would be here for me. I would not be alone now.

Within the hour, George called back to say he and Ann had gotten plane reservations for early the next morning and would be flying from San Diego International Airport into Seattle-Tacoma International. Sea-Tac is about thirty minutes south of Seattle if there is no traffic. Their flight would arrive in Seattle at approximately 9:45 a.m., and then they would take a taxi to my house and be there between eleven and twelve o'clock. I quickly explained why I wasn't offering to pick them up at the airport. My long-standing, morbid fear of driving on freeways did not bode well for such a trip. They understood. They were so kind to me.

As I look back over those sketchy notes I wrote in my appointment book for Friday, I see that, in the afternoon, I went for a cup of tea with an upstairs neighbor and then to a scheduled workout session with my trainer at the gym. I vaguely remember doing those things and looking back, I feel as if I had been sleepwalking. The next notes in the book, written late Friday evening, read, "7 p.m. to 9:15. Sat with Kevin at the hospital. Very bad." That was the best I could do.

***

At around six-thirty that evening, I arrived at the University of Washington Medical Center's main hospital campus and parked in a dizzying, multilevel underground parking garage across the street from the main entrance. I made it out of the garage without getting too lost, crossed the busy street, and walked up the cement steps to the main entrance and through the wide automatic glass doors. I still felt like I was moving in slow motion. At the front desk, I asked how to reach the cardiac intensive care unit. I think it was on the fourth floor. I took the elevator up. When I told the nurse at the cardiac unit front desk who I was and that I was there to see Kevin Boggs, she said, of course, she'd have Catherine come get me.

Catherine, the physician assistant, was a tall, slender woman in her thirties with her dark-blond hair pulled back into a neat ponytail. I think the medical shirt and scrubs she was wearing were beige, and she looked every bit the willowy, beautiful young nurse on an afternoon hospital soap opera. She did not smile but greeted me warmly. I followed her down the quiet hallway. I was aware that I couldn't feel my feet. About halfway down the hall, Catherine turned back to me and said, "Why don't we go find a quiet room first so we can talk?" I nodded and followed her a little farther down the hall and into a tiny room with a small wooden table and a couple of chairs, a counter and sink, a few supply cabinets, and a phone on the wall. I remember these details vividly. She beckoned me to sit down, and I did. *This is not happening,* I thought. *This is a dream…a very, very bad dream.* My head started to throb.

I remember Catherine explaining to me in simple terms that the infection that was discovered in Kevin's blood was called sepsis, and it had been too aggressive to halt by the time he had been taken back to Northwest. The infection had traveled through his blood, and his body's efforts to fight it off had resulted in serious injury to his organs, "causing them to become unstable." His kidneys, other organs, and finally, his heart had been damaged so quickly and irreparably that there was simply no chance he would survive. The doctors and nurses had done all they could. She asked if I had any questions. I said no. I could feel my heart exploding into a swirling, jagged mass of glass slivers inside my chest.

"All right then, you can come see him now if you like." Catherine stood and I followed her into Kevin's room. It was a cramped, private room with one long, narrow bed. I remember thinking the room looked hardly bigger than Kevin's walk-in closet at home. The body I saw stretched out on the bed was so still. His hands and fingers and lips and cheeks, his whole body—every part of him—was swollen, as if he had stumbled into a hive of maddened stinging bees. His eyes were closed, his face was sheet-white, and his long body barely fit the length of the bed. This person looked a little bit like Kevin, but this was not

Kevin. It *could* not be him. If it *was* his body lying here—and I knew it was—he must surely have left it already. I wondered if his spirit might be hovering somewhere near the ceiling, observing all this from above. I did not dare look up to see if it was true. I wasn't ready.

Catherine had been right when she'd told me Kevin was hooked up to multiple IVs, tubes and machines. A breathing tube had been inserted through his mouth down into his throat and was taped to his cheeks. All these contraptions were keeping his heart beating, keeping him hydrated, and as comfortable as possible. This was all they could do now.

A petite, young intensive care nurse, whose name I cannot remember, was in the room, moving methodically, checking the monitors, the IV lines, and the tubes, doing the things that intensive care nurses do. She stopped and smiled kindly at me. She must have been in her early twenties; her skin was as smooth as porcelain, and she wore her straight, platinum-blond hair in a stylish bob. She reminded me of a 1920s silent movie starlet. I noticed all these details too. *Where do they find these exquisite-looking people?* I wondered.

She told me I could touch Kevin and talk to him, but he probably would not respond. For a moment, I was not deterred. *I can do this*, I thought. *If I say the right thing, he'll wake up. He'll open his eyes and smile at me and say, "Hey, Rosie! Where have you been? I'm so glad to see you. Can we go home now? We have a Scrabble rematch to play."*

I had never touched Kevin in the seven months he had lived with me—except for our frequent fist bumps and high-fives. Now, I sat down in a chair next to his bed, lifted his cool, limp hand, and cradled it in mine. We had never had a reason to discuss what kind of women he was attracted to, but I thought I'd give it a try.

"Kevin, it's Rosie," I said. "You know, your nurse here is gorgeous, and you have to wake up so you can see her! And, you have to wake up anyway, 'cause you have to get better and come home." I nodded toward the young nurse, and she smiled at me. I was pleading with Kevin, and I was serious. But it didn't work. He did not open his eyes or say my name. There was no response. He remained still.

I stayed with Kevin for a bit longer, murmuring to him, occasionally touching his cheek, and stroking his forehead. I told him Jasmine missed him, I missed him, and that his parents were coming in the morning. Finally, I told him I had to go, and I left the room.

***

It was about 9:30 p.m. when I walked out the front door of the hospital. The sky was black. The night air was cool now, and the street was quiet. I sat down on the topmost of the wide concrete steps that led down to the street and the parking garage. Like the night and the street, I needed to be quiet. I could not make my mind move beyond the moment I was in or think how I would make my legs move or maneuver those steps down to the street and across it into the parking garage.

Instead, I pulled my iPhone out of my purse and called Ami—the very same Ami who had tried—and finally did—persuade me years ago to write the "Essential Roomie" book. Ami was about a year older than me and was tall and lissome with wild, frizzy blond hair. She was a singer-songwriter and guitarist. Soon after we met, we bonded over the mutual revelation that I could sing in perfect harmony with her by ear, my warm alto to her liquid soprano. We soon had what we called our "side gig," which simply meant that during Seattle's cloudless, blue-sky summer weather, we would occasionally go out and stand together on Capital Hill's neighborhood street corners and sing for the passersby, with Ami's guitar case set open on the sidewalk in front of us for tips. We got lots of quarters and even a few dollar bills.

Our "Carnegie Hall" moment was when, on one of those bright, sunny days, we took the bus downtown to Seattle's number-one tourist destination, Pike Place Market, and stood singing the Everly Brothers and Bonnie Rait to the crowds of curious people bustling by. We got smiles, nods, thumbs-up, and spare change that day. The fact that we never made any real money didn't matter; we were singing for the smiles and the joy of it. We even did a few parties and wedding gigs. Our official duo's name was Ami and Me, so we would both have top billing. We loved that.

Ami had been living in Tucson now for many years with her beloved longtime life partner, Mark. She had lost him quietly and without warning back in February of 2021, just about five months earlier, in the early morning hours of his seventy-first birthday. Mark had a bad heart and had worn a pacemaker for several years, but only recently had had a cardiac checkup, and his doctor was pleased. Everything looked great. And then, he went to bed and never woke up.

During those first months after Mark died, Ami and I had been talking on the phone almost every day, and more recently, at least once or twice a week. My heart was broken for her, and I was doing my best to support her through her shock and grief. When Kevin got sick that last Sunday, I had told her what was going on, and she had made me promise to keep her posted. She knew I was going to the hospital tonight.

Now, when I heard her voice on the phone, I croaked out, "Hey, Ami, it's me."

"Yes, sweetie, I'm here," she said. Her voice was low and kind, so full of love and patience and hopeful expectation. That was my Ami.

"I have to tell you something…they're saying Kevin's gonna die!"

"Oh, sweetie," Ami said.

"Yeah, this is not what I was expecting. This is *awful*," I said.

"Oh, I know, it's a big shock…he's meant a lot to you," Ami whispered.

Then I started to cry.

Ami comforted me while I sobbed. When we hung up, I dragged my body across the street, down into the parking garage, and eventually located my car. In a fog of despair, I slowly drove home.

Chapter Eight

The Last Weekend

THE NEXT MORNING, on Saturday, June 5, 2021, George texted me from Sea-Tac Airport that he and Ann had arrived. At exactly 11:15 a.m., a black-and-yellow taxi eased up to the curb in front of my condominium building in North Seattle. I had been waiting in the small lobby next to the bank of mailboxes when I saw the taxi arrive. I dashed outside, and as I approached the vehicle, I saw George and Ann Boggs climb out, each grasping a small, black wheeled suitcase.

I had not previously met Kevin's parents in person, but I had become friendly with them over the months since he'd moved in with me, bending my goofiest smile into a corner of Kevin's computer screen on an occasional Sunday, when he stood at the kitchen counter and Zoomed with them in California. They were funny, gracious, and good-natured toward me from that first meeting. They were glad Kevin was happy, that he had found such a welcoming home, and that he and I got along so well. I was happy they were happy, and Kevin was happy they were happy. It was a grand lovefest all around.

Now, George and Ann stood in front of me on the sidewalk. They made a handsome couple; both were in their late seventies, slender and tall. Ann was a smidgeon taller than George at almost six feet. They looked like a typical, mild-mannered Midwest-college professor and wife; George had on horn-rimmed glasses and wore a beige collared shirt, a patterned sweater vest, and a lightweight tweed jacket, and his slacks looked perfectly pressed. Ann's short, wavy, golden-auburn hair was cut in a stylish, conservative style, and she wore a Hillary Clinton–style pantsuit and low heels. She reminded me instantly of Carol Burnett, with comic timing in her eyes that promised an almost-but-not-quite bawdy joke at any moment, but I could see there would be no jokes today. The two of them looked so fragile, as if they were not sure where they were and what to do next. *Well, that makes total sense*, I thought. *They must be wondering how in the world they landed in this moment in this place. And I cannot help them.* I had no answers. I was as lost as they were. But being lost together was better than being lost alone.

Ann and George set their suitcases down on the sidewalk, and George leaned forward and hugged me. I could feel the gentle, firm pressure of his hands on my back as he squeezed me. I imagined him saying, "We're here now, Rosie. We are in pain, but we are all going to get through this together." Ann's hug lasted not quite a split second, and her eyes and body communicated, "I am the matter-of-fact one. You won't see my emotions, but don't worry, I have them. That's just who I am. It's the way I do things." And there was Kevin's kind gaze in both his parents' eyes. This deep, penetrating kindness pulled me in and swaddled me in that warm and welcoming way I knew so well from their oldest son. On a normal day, their eyes would have been twinkling, too, like Kevin's. Today, along with the kindness, I could see their fear and a fierce, desperate hope for a miracle.

"Thank you, Rosie. This is so kind—we appreciate it so much," George said as he and Ann rolled their small suitcases behind them, following me into the building's lobby and to the elevator.

"It's the least I can do," I said. "I'm just so glad you're here." It was true. I was deeply relieved. But my relief was shrouded in angst and despair. It was a surreal, out-of-body experience. *What* are *they doing here?* my brain asked. I knew the answer. They were here because Kevin was dying—was going to die. This was too much to handle. I asked about their flight, and we went upstairs.

George and Ann commented on how cute and comfy my condo looked, with its many books and stuffed animals and colorful art on the walls—and so many paintings and sketches and tchotchkes of cats everywhere—and they said they understood why Kevin and Jasmine had appreciated such a lovely environment. I felt a flush of gratitude and thanked them. I got them settled in Kevin's room, showed them how to adjust the thermostat and the shower controls, got them fresh towels, and made them each a mug of tea. Then we were on our way to the hospital. We were all quiet in the car, but it wasn't an awkward silence. But it was like we were embarking on a "mystery tour" with an undisclosed destination. George and Ann paid close attention to the streets we took so they could find their way back and forth to the hospital on their own. I reminded them they could use the navigation app on their phones, and they looked visibly relieved.

***

When I dropped Kevin's parents off at the entrance to the hospital, it was about 12:30 p.m. I drove directly home, but I have no recollection of how I spent the rest of the afternoon. It is how I imagine a person would experience a memory gap after an alcoholic blackout, but I don't drink, so I had no such excuse. It was grief and shock. I knew that. I do recall George texted me a few times to let me know that Kevin remained the same. George said that he and Ann wanted to take me out to dinner that night; we agreed that I would pick them up at the hospital around 6:30 and we'd go to Masala of India near my house, a favorite quiet restaurant of mine—one that, in fact, Kevin and I had frequented occasionally. It felt safe and appropriate for that night's meal. With its casually elegant décor, deep-burgundy walls, red cushioned booths, muted lighting, and kind waiters, the environment was calming. The sizzling aromas of cinnamon, curry, and green cardamom in the air added comfort to the calm.

George and Ann were waiting at the hospital entrance for me when I drove up, and they looked haggard. The ride to the restaurant was quiet, and dinner was quiet, too, but again, I felt no awkwardness. Instead, I felt at ease with them, as if I had known them forever. And now I was tethered to them by a yoke of unconditional love and appreciation for Kevin. My body let go a bit from the unspeakable emptiness of the moment. Over dinner, they spoke mostly of Kevin's life before I knew him, including his love for wood crafting, glass blowing, and cats; his raucous sense of humor; and stories of his wilder, unmoored times and periods of difficult searching. And, through it all was woven the thread of his kind heart.

Back home, George and Ann thanked me again for my kind hospitality and for being so good to Kevin.

"He's been so happy here," they said.

They planned to be up early Sunday morning; they would drive Kevin's car to the hospital and remain for as long as they needed to be there. We said goodnight and hugged at the doorway to Kevin's room. I saw Jasmine look up from her sleeping spot on Kevin's bed and thought I could see her smiling. She seemed happy to see them, and they looked happy to have her there with them. When they closed the door, I was overwhelmed by another flood of gratitude that they were here with me and with Jasmine, and that Jasmine would have the comforting presence of these Boggs humans in bed again tonight. But my gratitude remained achingly interwoven with despair and desolation that gnawed at my insides. Yes, they were here with me and with Kevin. Yet Kevin was not here among us and would not be coming home. It was unbelievable, and I was alone. Or would be soon enough. Without my friend. Without Kevin Boggs, this tall, gangly, funny, kind man. Alone, again. But not yet.

On Sunday morning, George and Ann were up and out of the condo by nine to go back to the hospital. They took Kevin's car. I wasn't completely awake yet, but I heard them go. Throughout the rest of the morning and afternoon, George texted me as he and Ann sat on either side of Kevin's bed, holding their oldest son's hands and talking brokenly and soothingly to him. They talked and talked to Kevin during those last long hours. They told me later that they could not tell if he was hearing or understanding them, but they wanted him to know how much they had always loved him. They kept me in the loop via text messages the whole time. I was amazed and humbled by their efforts, and I was terrified of what was to come—a huge black nothingness. There would be no more Kevin.

Around 3 p.m., George sent one more text. It read, *Rosie, we can't leave for a while longer. Kevin is fading quickly.* I stared at the words on the phone, and then I bent forward, clutched my stomach, and sobbed.

As usual, I don't have much of a memory for what else happened after that. Sometime on Tuesday, I had called Kevin's friend Caitlin to tell her he was sick. On Saturday, I'd called again and she was flabbergasted when I described what was happening. She said she couldn't believe Kevin hadn't let her know when he got so sick.

"You probably don't know I used to be a nurse, Rosie," Caitlin had explained. "I could have done something!" My heart had thudded into my stomach. *She could have helped. But it was too late now. Too late.*

Caitlin had asked me to keep her posted. Now, after reading George's text, I called her again as promised, and I asked her if she wanted to— would be willing to—come to my house to be with me and Kevin's parents once they got home from the hospital. Without hesitation, Caitlin said yes but asked me to get permission from George and Ann first. She knew them, and they knew her, and that she was a longtime cherished friend of Kevin's, but they had never met in person, and she didn't want to be in the way. I texted George while we spoke, and he responded instantly. *Yes, please, Rosie, thank you. We would very much like to see her.*

I told Caitlin, and she promised to come. Then, as I had rehearsed, I said, "Caitlin, you know Jasmine, of course, Kevin's cat. I think you know her…and you have cats—or a cat—and a dog yourself, right?"

I didn't have time to take a breath. "Rosie, I will be happy to take Jasmine, if that's what you're asking me," Caitlin said. "It will be fine. Yes, I know Jasmine, and she knows my critters. In fact, she and Kevin stayed with me for a few weeks a while back when he needed a place to stay."

Relief surged through me, and tears welled up in my eyes. "Yes, please, Caitlin. That is exactly it. I love Jasmine and I would keep her in a second, but I have Sadie, and there's no way it would work…but I couldn't just give her to a stranger…"

"Rosie, it's fine. It's perfect. I'll be over soon, and we'll talk more about it then," Caitlin said. "It'll be fine, I promise."

Then I texted George back. *That would be lovely. She'd like to see you too. And she said she can take Jasmine indefinitely, if necessary. Jasmine already knows her and her dog and cat.*

***

At about 4 p.m., George texted me one last time from the hospital. The text read, *Kevin is gone.* More incomprehensible words stared out at me from the screen of my iPhone, and I thought I could hear sounds—like skyscrapers exploding and collapsing around Kevin's parents' shoulders as they sat huddled together at their child's bedside in the hospital room, with nothing but ashes settling at their feet.

When George and Ann got home from the hospital around 6:30 that evening, I did not know what to do with my brain and my body as they walked through the condo door. I reached out and hugged them both, and I think I whimpered something like "I'm so sorry." Caitlin arrived soon after. We all hugged again. We sat close together in the living room, talking softly. I tried to remember how to breathe. I offered water and tea.

Caitlyn and I listened as George and Ann talked about their last hours with Kevin.

"At some point," George said, "Kevin's doctor came in and told us that Kevin wouldn't make it through the night...and that if we wanted to be with him when he died, we would have to remove his life support." (Some months later, George wrote in a letter to me: "This was the most difficult moment of my life, Rosie...I remember Ann leaning toward Kevin to tell him, 'The doctor says you have to leave us now—we love you.' It still brings tears to my eyes.")

I could see a grayish light hovering in the air around us, filled with our stunned pain, disbelief, and exhaustion, and of Kevin's sweet presence and his stark absence—his being forever gone. Caitlin reconfirmed her promise to take Jasmine. She and I would talk later in the week to make plans for her to retrieve Jasmine.

Once Caitlin said good-bye, George and Ann stood up, holding hands and looking at each other. "Well, we should probably...start going through Kevin's things," George said. We hugged again. He and Ann walked together into Kevin's bedroom. Looking at their backs as they walked away from me, I felt my heart explode again into a million pieces. I thought, *How many times can one person's heart shatter? This feels like the worst moment so far. But what about all the ones to come? Oh God, this cannot be happening. Kevin is gone—forever.* I thought about getting something to eat, but I wasn't hungry. My stomach was as hard and knotted as a clenched fist.

I checked in occasionally with George and Ann that evening. Jasmine was still curled on Kevin's bed with her eyes half closed, seemingly content to be with George and Ann as they began sorting through Kevin's things, making piles for keeping, washing, packing, donating, and disposing. George asked me for some notepaper so they could start making a list of all the things they would have to accomplish the next day.

There was so much to be done and so many phone calls to make—to Kevin's boss, his volunteer coordinator, the Social Security Administration, and the investment manager. They would have to find a funeral home in Seattle that could take Kevin's body and make arrangements for his cremation and the recovery of his ashes. And, they'd have to figure out when and how and who (George, of course, with one of their two other sons, which one not yet decided) would drive back up to Seattle with George's Toyota pickup truck to take care of the rest of Kevin's furniture and belongings. At least George and Ann would be able to fly back to California on their confirmed return flight on Tuesday morning. They were relieved to know that Jasmine had a new family with a good human and furry critters she knew. But first, they had to call home and tell the other boys and their families that Kevin was gone.

I didn't see much of George and Ann the next day. They were busy with sorting and long phone conversations. They took a break to shop for a few groceries, eat a little lunch, and fill me in on what they were finding out. That night, the three of us went back to Masala for dinner. I heard more stories of Kevin, some raucously funny, some heartrending, and some simply sweet in their extraordinary ordinariness.

George talked about his own long career as a university professor, and he and Ann told me about the rest of their family, the kids, the grandkids, and their house in rural San Diego County. They described the several-acre vegetable and fruit-tree garden that George tended, and how, in addition to being a master woodworker, he was a master baker. His most locally famous and sought-after creation was his key lime pie. I would remember this part of the conversation with another rush of that now familiar Boggs-bestowed gratitude a few short weeks later when he and his son Ian would arrive back in Seattle, emerge from George's Toyota truck, and greet me on the curb, with George shyly placing a package, meticulously wrapped in brown paper, into my hands. "This is for you, Rosie," he said then. "This is one of my famous key lime pies. Because I remember you said how much you liked them."

Oddly, or maybe not so oddly, I don't remember seeing Kevin's parents off on Tuesday morning. They had to leave my place at around 7 a.m. to get to the airport, and as you know, this is not my favorite time of day to be awake under any circumstances. This time, however, it's more likely that I could not have borne saying good-bye again. I'm sure we did that the night before. That's the way it must have happened.

CHAPTER NINE

Heat Wave—
in the Aftermath

DURING THE NEXT COUPLE of weeks, George and I talked on the phone a few times, and Ann got on the phone briefly during just one of those calls. She said she was fine. While she sounded okay, George told me she wasn't eating much, and he was worried about her. So was I.

George and Ian, Kevin's next-youngest brother, were making plans to drive back up to Seattle at the end of June. With George's pickup truck and Kevin's SUV, which remained in the garage of my building, they would be able to go through the remainder of Kevin's things, pack what they wanted to take home in both cars, and mini-caravan back to California.

By the end of June, Seattle was wilting under a rare, humid heat wave that extended up and down the West Coast with tongue-panting temperatures in the 90s day and night. George and Ian left Southern California in the late morning of Saturday, June 26, intending to stop for the night about halfway along to break up the approximately eighteen-and-a-half-hour drive from San Marcos to Seattle. But because of the heat wave, they could find no motel with a vacancy. Too many folks had decided to camp out temporarily in every remaining air-conditioned motel and hotel room along the Oregon coast. There would be no place to stop and rest in the middle of this heat. I cringed at the irony of that. This dilemma felt indistinguishable to me from the consuming heat wave of grief I was enveloped in. There was no safe place for me to rest, to find peace. This was a perfect storm of catastrophe. This was hell.

So George and Ian drove straight through, stopping only for snacks, bathroom breaks, and to stretch their legs. They texted me at intervals. Around midnight, George texted again to say that their ETA at that point was around five the next morning. He assured me that he and Ian could hang out in the car or at a coffee shop once they reached Seattle until I was up and about; they did not want to disturb me. He was so sweet—so George—so Boggs.

Don't worry about it, George, I texted back. As you know well now, dear reader, I am rarely asleep at midnight anyway, and this night I had no plans or capacity to be asleep at five in the morning. One o'clock, three o'clock, five o'clock? It made no difference to me. Whether it was my routine night-owlish habits, the heat, the grief, the anxiously eager anticipation of George and Ian's arrival, or a combination of everything, I knew I would be wide-awake.

I dozed a little, read, and wandered around the condo. When George and Ian arrived at exactly 5 a.m., they called me from George's pickup truck, and I ran downstairs to meet them. The day was just dawning. There they stood, on the curb next to George's big maroon truck with its long camper shell. It looked *so* big, big enough to carry all of Kevin's things away. *What a striking jewel tone color,* I thought absent-mindedly. One of my favorites. When they saw me, their shy smiles emerged. I went to them. That was when George handed me the carefully wrapped key lime pie—the famous made-from-scratch pie he had shyly described over dinner at Masala of India when he and Ann were here. That warm flush of appreciation, of feeling loved and cared for, coursed through me. At the same time, those same slivers of my broken heart were hurtling around inside my chest again.

George introduced me to Ian, and we all hugged. George and Ian were both dressed in flannel shirts and jeans. Their shirts were wrinkled and they looked completely worn out. Ian stood as wide, tall, and solid as a football linebacker. Later, George told me that Ian is six feet eight, even taller than Kevin's six feet four. But in that moment, I saw only that this younger brother was indeed a gentle giant, with Kevin's same kind eyes and wide grin.

I opened the garage door with my remote and guided them inside to park George's pickup behind my car. They unloaded their suitcases, and I escorted them upstairs and got them settled in Kevin's bedroom—I had tidied up again, of course, and put clean sheets on the bed after George and Ann had flown home in early June. And then I left father and son to sleep for a few hours. I tried to sleep, too. But my heart hurt from the shock of having looked into the face of yet another Boggs brother with Kevin's same soft, pale skin, a smooth-shaven head, and twinkly eyes, now so somber. Here were all the familiar Boggs genes, alive and well in the bodies of both father and second son, now resting in Kevin's bedroom in Kevin's bed. But there was no Kevin. How could that possibly be? Where was he? The incongruity gave me a headache. I finally fell asleep, too.

Once George and Ian were up and around, I made lunch for us— tuna fish sandwiches with not too much mayonnaise (the way Kevin liked it), dark, leafy green lettuce and red onion, and the salt-free potato chips (a concession to me) I always had on hand. I made Ian's sandwich supersized like Kevin's. Father and son drank two of the cold drinks they had brought in the car, a Snapple iced tea for George and a Coke Zero for Ian.

The rest of the day, I leaned my head periodically into Kevin's room and meandered in and out, doing my best to be helpful. George and Ian spent hours sorting what was still left of Kevin's belongings, looking through, organizing, and separating them into piles: some to pack and take home to San Marcos, some to donate to Goodwill, and a few more things to throw out. There was Kevin's six-and-a-half-foot-long, red plaid–upholstered couch with its heavy, wood-framed arms and back— much too large and cumbersome to fit into their station wagon or to deliver to Goodwill. We called a student-owned and operated hauling truck service that promised to pick it up later that week. George and Ian looked at Kevin's almost brand-new, extra-long, queen-size bed with its sturdy Purple brand mattress and metal bed frame, then looked at each other. Then George pronounced that it could stay with me. I said thank you. I was grateful. George had bought that bed for Kevin as a gift when he moved into the condo. It was a perfect bed. It was Kevin's bed. That night, we all retired early. It had been a long day.

***

On Monday, June 28, George and Ian set off to complete their first brutal task of the day—going to the funeral home to pick up Kevin's ashes and his official death certificate. They graciously declined my offer to go with them. "It's not necessary, Rosie. Why don't you skip this? Just stay home and rest."

Rest, I thought. *That's a good one.* But I was grateful for the respite. I did not want to go. The thought of it threw me into a frenzy of fear. When they returned, they walked in quietly. George held Kevin's ashes in a tall, plain, dark-bronze metal urn. I looked at the urn. Then George handed me Kevin's death certificate. I looked at the words on the official-looking paper. There was his name. Kevin Dale Boggs, date of death, June 6, 2021. *How can this be?* I thought. *This is all wrong. It makes no sense.* Yet it was true. I felt my heart split open again, spilling out another avalanche of razor-sharp bits of glass inside my chest. *How many more times? Five, ten, a dozen times? A million? Every day for the rest of my life?*

I felt nauseous, and the room swam a little. *Damn it, Rosie, get a grip.* I thought I could hear Blanche hissing at me from a distance. I put the paper down on the kitchen table, looked into George and Ian's sad eyes, and excused myself. I walked into my bedroom, crawled onto the bed, and curled my body into a tight ball with my arms wrapped around my stomach. I think I fell asleep for a while.

Their second task that day was to go meet Bert, the director of peer counseling, where Kevin had been a mentor to other recovering addicts. George told me that night how much Bert had appreciated Kevin's devotion to his mentoring role, and how she and Kevin's counselees were shocked and saddened when they heard Kevin had died. Bert wanted George and Ian to know this, to know that she was deeply moved by their visit when they had so much else to think about, and that she was honored to meet them.

George and Ian arrived home around 4 p.m. They rested a bit, and then we went out to an early dinner at Masala again. It was now officially our Rosie-Boggs "favorite safe place" to eat. It had become our refuge.

Our conversation was subdued during dinner, but as it had been with George and Ann, I felt no awkwardness. Instead, I was overwhelmed by a swaddling sensation of deep comfort, having these two Boggs men sitting with me and holding me in their hearts; they were Kevin's flesh and blood, so solid and kind, so physical and alive—here with me, helping keep the earth firm under my feet—for now.

The next day, their last one with me, was again busy. In the morning, George, Ian, and I took the last of Kevin's things to the Goodwill where Kevin and I had spent our occasional Sunday afternoons together rummaging for flannel shirts and shoes. My chest ached. *Why are we donating these things?* I thought. *They are Kevin's things. He just bought some of them. He might still* need *them. And why is he not in the car? Why is he not here? Where is he?* And, then the same echo from Blanche—"What is *wrong* with you, Rosie? Get with it and stop being so self-absorbed. These two men need you." I watched from what felt like a great distance away as George and Ian solemnly handed Kevin's things to the drop-off men.

Then we went grocery shopping for a few things to have for dinner at home that night. In the early afternoon, George drove us in his pickup truck down to Vigor Shipyards. George had called Kevin's boss, Bill Phillips, the day before, and Bill, without a moment of hesitation, invited us down to meet him and Kevin's workmates, saying he would give us the grand tour of the shipyard. When George hesitated, Bill said that if we were up to it, he had plenty of time and we would not be in the way.

At the entrance gate to the shipyard, Bill greeted the three of us with unabashed bear hugs and a wide smile that lit up his rough, kindly face. He was tall, broad, and burly with short gray hair on his round head and his two upper front teeth missing. His face and arms were deeply tanned and weather-worn from years of hard work and possible heartache; he reminded me instantly of a tall-ship captain from the 1800s. Bill handed each of us a shiny white plastic safety hard hat for visitors. Then he did as he had promised, walking us around the vast shipyard grounds to gaze up at the massive ferries and ships docked there, pointing out the ones Kevin had worked on. Bill shared stories of how Kevin had been adored and respected by his workmates because of his patience, fairness, and wacky sense of humor.

As we walked, I felt that same eerie, incongruous sensation enveloping me—that something was terribly askew in this picture. After all,

Kevin had talked about one day taking me on a tour of the shipyard, and here it was happening. But instead of Kevin, it was his dad and brother walking side by side with me across the grounds, marveling at the big ships and Kevin's capacity to do this grueling and demanding work. And recalling his kindness. Oh yes, Kevin was a role model, Bill said. He'd worked hard and well and had a maturity that was not easy to find.

When Bill took us inside the main building that housed the employee canteen, lockers, and spacious lounge, we found a ragtag line of Kevin's coworkers who had gathered to meet us. They reminded me of the Seven Dwarfs, except there were more of them, all standing in a crooked row—at least twenty, I guessed—disheveled in their oil- and dirt-stained coveralls, shifting their feet back and forth and looking pleased, sad, and sheepish. I felt like Snow White, standing gratefully before them. *Maybe they're thinking I'll wave a magic wand and bring Kevin back*, I thought. But I could not grant their wish. Instead, George, Ian, and I walked slowly down the line, shaking their work-roughened hands, asking them their names, and murmuring thank-yous. I thought I could feel my heart literally begin to tremble inside my chest.

Okay, I thought, when I couldn't catch my breath, *it could be a heart attack. Nah, pretty sure it's a panic attack. Cuz this has to be the hardest part of this visit for me.* But it got worse. I sighed off and on to keep my breath moving. After that, Bill walked with us to Kevin's work locker, a tall, narrow metal locker standing among dozens of others. Bill said he had wanted to wait to open it until we were there. He took a key from his pocket, unlocked the padlock, and opened the door. Inside was a scattered assortment of small tools, papers, maps, and pens. A pair of worn beige-leather work boots sat on the floor, and hanging on a hook was a pair of tattered leather work overalls with a few burn holes in the legs. And on a shelf at the top of the locker rested two hard hats. The first was one of the white plastic visitor hard hats, and the second—obviously Kevin's—was made of rust-colored heavy plastic, full of dents and covered in faded Vigor Shipyard stickers. It looked as if it had been through several wars. I thought it looked lonely. Bill gently lifted it down from the shelf and held it out toward us. Yes, this was Kevin's, the one he wore every day at work.

"I thought one of you might like this," he said.

"I would." I heard the faint words and realized they were my own. I looked up at George and at Ian and saw them both smiling at me, their eyes looking sad and tender.

"It's fine, Rosie. You take it," George said. I took the hard hat from Bill, staring at it, feeling its weight in my hands. I thought, *Okay, I get it. This is the hardest part.*

Then Bill said, "You can have the visitor hard hat too if you'd like it, Rosie." I touched the white one on my head that Bill had given each of us when we had arrived. "No, I'll keep the one I'm wearing, if it's okay."

***

That evening, George, Ian, and I had a simple dinner at home, and they finished packing the last remaining items into their two vehicles. I don't remember what we ate or if I slept much that night.

In the morning, I made breakfast, and afterward it was time to go. We hugged a few more times, and these two dear Boggs men thanked me for the millionth time for my kindness and hospitality, and for what a good friend I had been to Kevin. Down in the garage, I watched as they loaded their suitcases into George's truck along with two large brown paper grocery bags filled with snacks, drinks, and sandwiches we had prepared for the road. We hugged one more time. This time, I wanted all the hugs I could get. Remembering how Kevin and I had never hugged, I was eager to stock up. Then George got into the driver's seat of his truck, and Ian folded himself into Kevin's blue SUV. I clicked open the garage door with my remote and guided them out of the parking garage and into the street, now busy with rush-hour traffic, so they could begin their trip home.

Okay, now, this *is it,* I thought. *This is the hardest part. It's gotta be. How can it get any worse?* But then, once again, it did. I stood on the sidewalk and watched them drive away. After both their cars were out of sight, I stood for a few more minutes in the sweltering heat. More pain was coming. I could feel it in my body—so much more. So, I stood still and tried to find my breath and waited for the ground to rip open beneath my feet and swallow me whole. Part of me was hoping—wishing—pleading it would happen.

Nothing.

And then, I heard myself—or maybe it was Blanche—yeah, it was her again, saying, "Oh Rosie, for Pete's sake, what is *wrong* with you? I keep telling you. The worst is over now—you'll be all right. So—finish up your grieving and get on with your life."

I tried to get on with both. I really did. I was doing the best I could.

Part II

***

Disenfranchised Grief—
What It Is and
Why It Matters

CHAPTER TEN

Words from the Experts

As YOU KNOW, during my exploration back into the grief literature (yes, YouTube included!), I discovered Dr. Kenneth Doka and the term *disenfranchised grief*. I have since discovered that most all the research, exploration, and discussion of the concept of disenfranchised grief through the present day—including what is in my book—is grounded in the thoughts presented in Doka's comprehensive and now classic 1989 book, *Disenfranchised Grief: Recognizing Hidden Sorrow.*

The book, edited by Doka, is a compilation of work by him and other leading researchers and mental health-care professionals. "The chapters in this book reflect five years of developing and exploring the concept of disenfranchised grief."[4] In Chapter One, Doka defines disenfranchised grief "as the grief that persons experience when they incur a loss that is not or cannot be openly acknowledged, publicly mourned, or socially supported."[5]

Doka states in the book's introduction that its core message is "the hope that, by helping people to recognize such losses, support may be made more available to the bereaved, and their pain understood and thereby lessened."[6] That's my hope too in writing *this* book; I believe the message is as valid today as it was then.

Learning this term literally saved my life, at least my emotional life, as you know; it helped me understand and accept, if not lessen, my pain. It gave me permission to shed the shame, to begin to honor all my feelings, and to hold Kevin tenderly in my heart as I grieved the loss of him. In this chapter, I discuss some of the basic nuts and bolts of disenfranchised grief as expressed by Doka and other disenfranchised grief experts who have come after him. Let us dive in once more.

HELPFUL DEFINITIONS

Acknowledge: To recognize the rights, status, or authority of; to recognize as genuine or valid.[7]

Bereavement: The loss of a loved one by death.[8]

Disenfranchise: To deprive of a franchise, of a legal right or privilege.[9]

Disenfranchised grief: As defined above by Doka, it is the grief people experience over a loss that they do not feel entitled to; "the loss cannot be openly acknowledged, socially validated, or publicly mourned."[10]

Grief: A deep and poignant distress caused by, *or as if by, bereavement* (my italics).[11]

Grieve: To feel or show grief over.[12]

Improper: Not suited to the circumstances; not in accordance with modesty, good manners, or good taste.[13]

Impropriety: The quality or state of being improper.[14]

Loss: (1) Destruction, ruin; (2) the act of losing possession; (3) the harm or privation resulting from loss or separation.[15]

Shame: (1) A painful emotion caused by consciousness of [or belief in (my words)] guilt, shortcoming, or impropriety; (2) a condition of humiliating disgrace or disrepute; (3) something that brings censure or reproach.[16]

Validate: To recognize, establish, or illustrate the worthiness or legitimacy of.[17]

LISA S. ZOLL, LCSW
PROFESSOR, AUTHOR, AND FOUNDER AND CLINICAL DIRECTOR
OF GRIEF RELIEF THERAPY, LLC (GRIEFRELIEFTHERAPY.COM)

One of the other most comprehensive and thought-provoking articles I found after discovering the concept of disenfranchised grief—and one that remains a personal favorite of mine—was called "Disenfranchised Grief: When Grief and Grievers Are Unrecognized," by Lisa S. Zoll, a licensed clinical social worker and the founder and clinical director of Grief Relief Therapy, LLC, which "specializes in helping clients challenged by loss, grief, and trauma."[18]

> Lisa developed an approach for how to look at the journey of grief that removed the stages, expectations, and timeframes, banishing the word closure. The approach is more about weaving your loss into your life and honoring your journey instead of treating it like a problem to be solved.[19]

In her article, published in the Winter 2018 issue of *The New Social Worker*, Zoll, whose clients include such often-disenfranchised grievers as first responders, talks from her extensive personal and professional experience and expertise about when grief is disenfranchised.[20] The fact that, in addition to everything else, she was an EMT (emergency medical technician) for six years and a volunteer firefighter did not hurt her credibility in my eyes!

Disenfranchised grief, Zoll states, is where, for the griever, the relationship between the grief and the loss goes unrecognized through discounting and disparaging behaviors, words, and attitudes of friends, family, and society at large. The loss is minimized, the grief is invalidated, and the griever is left doubting the validity of the grief itself.[21] *Damn,* I thought, *that is rough stuff.*

Zoll clarifies and defines inclusively the concept of loss that results in grief: "Loss, in this article, is defined as the disappearance of something cherished, such as a person or possession to which there is an emotional attachment or bond (Zoll & Shiner, 2017)."[22] Grief is the emotion that results from any such significant loss. And, Zoll stresses,

"Acknowledgment of a loss is intrinsic to the recovery process."[23] *All right! Touche, Lisa!*

Using her own case examples, Zoll elucidates on Doka's three reasons that can result in disenfranchised grief.[24]

The Griever Is Not Recognized

In her article, Zoll describes the experience of Shannon Wood, a ten-year-old girl whose best friend, ten-year-old Jen Shiner, and her eight-year-old brother Dave, were murdered by their father, their mother Lynn's ex-husband, "who then took his life. Lynn was the obvious griever."[25]

The article continues: "Wood felt isolated in her loss and believed that no one could fathom how she felt. Her proof was the silence she encountered on the topic of Jen's death. After the funeral, there was little recognition or acknowledgment that Wood had lost her best friend. Her grief quickly became disenfranchised, her fears invisible to others (S. Wood, personal communication, February 8, 2018)."[26]

When I read this, I gasped. In the twenty-first century, for any child protective-service social worker worth their MSW, this would have been an obvious and egregious failure of the care professionals, but I am sure that in the 1990s, any social workers involved in the case were woefully understaffed and busy with the mother of the murdered children and did not have the time or the official permission or responsibility to even inquire, much less tend to the emotional welfare of Jen's best friend, Shannon. There may have been no social services involved at all. Maybe it was just the homicide detectives. And what did they know then—or now—about helping those indirect survivors deal with such traumatic grief? That was not their job.

Thus, the social services and police enforcement systems could be forgiven for their ignorance. But then there were the families, the friends, and everyone else who did not seem to acknowledge Wood's loss. I suppose they could be forgiven, too. There simply was not much understanding of that idea then—that someone not directly related to a traumatic loss might be impacted by it. And, the concept of disenfranchised grief was not a "thing" yet. The very idea of it had existed only since 1989. And, to make the situation worse, Zoll states in the article that at the time of this murder, which occurred in 1994,[27] it was thought by many that "young children may be incapable of grieving or do not have the need to grieve (Corr, 1999). This example proves otherwise."[28] *Got it. Oh, my head.*

The Relationship Is Not Recognized

This case example is the story of a devoted foster couple who had to give up their two toddler foster daughters after the girls had been with them for only four months. The couple was preparing to adopt the children and had developed an affectionate and deeply bonded relationship with them. "At the custody hearing, the judge awarded custody to a distant relative of the biological mother."[29]

Wow. I can surmise that it might have been a happy ending for the biological relatives and hopefully for the children—but it certainly was not for the foster parents. They were devastated. No one seemed to notice, or that seemed to be the case, since no one acted to support them emotionally. The couple felt abandoned by even their closest friends and relations. "The response, 'At least, they got to be with you for that time' (M. & J. Schwartzman, personal communication, February 11, 2018), seemed to diminish the magnitude of their grief. Ten years later, that loss was still palpable to the couple."[30]

Wow, I can relate to that one. My thoughts returned to the dozens and dozens of foster families my fellow child-protective social workers and I had worked with at Catholic Charities in the '70s, who had foster children constantly come and go. Some went back to their birth parents, while some went to relatives, other foster homes, and institutions. Some aged out of the system and were on their own. I thought gratefully of the lucky foster families for whom the matches were necessary and of good quality, where the children were happy and got to stay for good, sometimes even ending in adoption. There were, of course, all the birth parents I had worked with who had to give up their children to those very foster homes temporarily, and yes, sometimes tragically, forever. The grief borne by the birth parents was given attention, and rightly so. But had we given the foster parents' grief enough attention? Probably not. Foster parents were supposed to be stronger than that, after all. Their grief was not a priority in the foster care system.

The Loss Is Not Recognized

This case example describes a kind of loss that is "stigmatized by society as 'not worthy' of grief."[31] This is when, for example, a person recovering from addictions must give up not only their addictive behavior, but also the people, places, and activities they depended on during their active addiction as they struggle to remain sober. This powerful idea will resonate with anyone who has ever been a part of a twelve-step community. Imagine all the loss and grief so often disregarded and disenfranchised by the larger community; thankfully, this grief can be acknowledged and processed in groups like Alcoholics Anonymous, Al-Anon Family Groups, Narcotics Anonymous, Overeaters Anonymous, Sex and Love Addicts Anonymous, and all the rest. That's one reason why all those tissue boxes and hot tea and coffee are provided at the meetings! The twelve-step world, thankfully, seems to have a handle on this stuff; in those rooms, all grief is recognized as real, valid, and deserving of loving attention and healing. I believe that while an individual twelve-stepper may not have heard of disenfranchised grief by its clinical name, they know it when they see it, and they make room for it.

***

Zoll's article sealed the deal for me. Nondeath-related grief and loss can be intense, like for those grieving foster parents, or subtle but equally intense, like for the recovering addict who grieves "the good ol' days." But, these losses and the grief that results are as real and valid as the grief over the death of a person. The fact remains that when the validity and importance of nondeath-related grief experiences are neglected and denied, the same great additional harm comes to the grievers. We are left to endure our grief alone without the ability to grieve openly, with the support of community and tradition and free from shame, and possibly without sufficient healing to allow for new, healthy relationships with people and things. Our normal and necessary grief is never processed and never healed, or not healed enough so that we can bear to carry it with us as a badge of love. It is sometimes literally banished from our consciousness. Thus, my need to shout it from the rooftops: Disenfranchised grief is real, and neglecting it can be deadly.

Of course, since Zoll was a social worker like me, I was eager to talk with her. I contacted her clinic and set up a phone visit. Sure enough, she greeted me warmly on the phone. We talked about disenfranchised grief, her practice, her writings, our lives as social workers, and my hope that my book-in-progress might help bring the idea of disenfranchised grief out of the shadows and onto the center stage of people's everyday lives. She gave me her blessing. *Social workers are such good people,* I thought, and I applauded myself for the millionth time for having chosen all those years ago to make social work my first career.

NIKKI MOBERLY, ICF, PCC, CBC
CERTIFIED MASTER END-OF-LIFE AND GRIEF COACH
In a 2021 article titled "Coping with Disenfranchised Grief: Five Steps to Start Healing," published on the online BetterUp blog, Nikki Moberly agrees with Doka. She states: "Disenfranchised grief is when your grieving doesn't fit into society's larger attitude about dealing with death and loss…No matter what type of loss you have experienced, your grief is valid. In the case of disenfranchised grief, this lack of social recognition and support can prolong the emotional pain related to grief. It adds another layer of complexity to an already-complicated grieving process."[32]

Okay, this is a juicy article too, I thought as I began to read. *I will probably be able to relate.*

In her article, Moberly describes five key themes of disenfranchised grief and five steps to begin healing. (You will find her healing steps options in Chapter Eighteen.) I took up my pencil to check off anything that rang a bell or, more aptly, hit a nerve—a tender, fragile nerve. It turns out, no surprise, that so very many of my nerves got jangled. I have put check marks and examples next to themes I recognized from my own life or from other people's lives that resonated deeply with me.

Moberly's five key themes of disenfranchised grief are connected by the fact that they "are rooted in social norms. Social norms establish expectations for grief reactions, mourning rites, and rituals. These may vary by society, religion, nationality, or other familial factors."[33]

Moberly's Five Themes of Disenfranchised Grief

1. **Lack of recognition for the importance of the relationship.** Moberly states, "Whether it's a rift or change in the relationship, loss of life, or changing dynamics, there are different types of relationships that can fall into this category."[34] This includes the following:

   a. **Infidelity.** Check! ✔ *Tom, my boyfriend from the '70s who betrayed me with a girl we both knew and who then wanted to come back to me. Yup, the same one who drove me to Boston in the U-Haul. I know, it's complicated.*

   Check! ✔ *My medical student boyfriend from my social work-student days, another beau who cheated on me with one of his fellow medical students; she was very pretty, which made it so much worse.*

   And, check. ✔ *How could I forget my husband, who cheated on me—not with a woman (I would have just killed him)—but with the money from his kids' college trust fund?*

   b. **Death of an ex-spouse.** Check! ✔ *Or an ex-spouse's relative (see Debi's story in Chapter Eighteen).*

   c. **Hidden or forbidden relationships.** Check! ✔ *All my gay friends who had to grieve their own friends and lovers and relatives suffering and dying of AIDS. (And, don't forget all the straight and other-gendered friends and family who have grieved in secret over those lost ones.)*

   d. **Loss of a close friend or neighbor who is like family.** Triple-whammy check! ✔ *Oh God, Kevin, there you are.*

2. **Cause of death surrounded by stigma.** This includes the following:

   a. **Suicide.** Check! ✔ *My reclusive first cousin Jay, who, at the age of sixty-nine, was still living—now alone—in his child-hood home in Boulder, Colorado, that he had shared with his mother (my maternal Aunt Helena) until her death in 2007. I had not seen Jay in decades. In 2015, he hanged himself in his bedroom. His younger sister, my cousin Joanne, found his body. I was not so concerned for myself but for Joanne. I did not think for a long time what it might mean for me.*

   b. **Drug overdose.** Check! ✔ *I am painfully aware of the people* *who have been left behind by the untimely and unnecessary deaths of their loved ones from an opioid or other drug overdose. These lost loved ones include everyone from corporate executives to unhoused and forgotten war veterans, queer teenagers, neglected children and grandparents, and all the others from every walk of life. The ones who are left behind, like the ones who have been lost, are all of us.*

3. **Social expectations for your grief journey.** Moberly states, "Societal norms and a general lack of understanding of the human experience around grief can lead to judgments from others."[35] This includes the following:
   a. **How long you grieve.** Check! ✓ *My cats and Kevin.*
   b. **How deeply you grieve.** Check! ✓ *My cats and Kevin.*
   c. **What emotions are considered appropriate.** And check again! ✓ *My cats and Kevin. Oh, my head hurts.*

4. **Losses considered less significant than others.** Moberly states, "Any kind of significant loss can cause a grief reaction. But some losses are deemed less worthy by societal standards, including many nondeath losses."[36] This includes the following:
   a. **Infertility.** Check! ✓ *My girlfriend Liza, who tried unsuccessfully for years to become pregnant. She never thought she had the right to grieve.*
   b. **Divorce.** Check! ✓ *My soulmate husband.*
   c. **Job loss.** Check! ✓ *Even if you quit.*
   d. **A life-changing diagnosis like Alzheimer's.** ✓ *Check! Several of my "little old ladies" and all those who must live with the thousand cuts of losing their loved ones over and over every day through the last day and beyond.*
   e. **The loss of a beloved pet.** Check a million times over! ✓ *Whether through the ache of separation—like having to surrender the cat because the rest of your family is allergic to it, or your rabbit going missing and never coming home, or through death—like your new kitten getting squashed to death by a stranger's car or your own car with you driving it, your wee*

dachshund getting eaten by a coyote out back, or having to go through compassionate euthanasia of your aged parakeet. Extra check marks for all my cats and my friends' and relatives' cats, dogs, birds, bunnies, hamsters, lizards, and more.

    f.   **The empty-nest syndrome when adult children leave the home.** *Check!* ✓ *My friend Savannah, whose only child, Grace, left for college and who, before and after her daughter's departure, was overwhelmed by grief and debilitating shame over her grief, because her daughter was "only about fifty miles away," and they talked every day. None of her grief felt valid in Savannah's eyes.*

    g.   **The end of an intimate relationship that is unformalized,** such as a romantic boyfriend or girlfriend (or any relationship with a significant other that falls outside the bounds of marriage or some other sanctified role). *Check!* ✓ *It's embarrassing (see how the shame wells up?) to admit how many of those endings there were for me over the years—all those boyfriends, sigh. But wait, how about the girlfriends? Platonic girlfriends, dearest and closest girlfriends, girlfriends who are like sisters, and the ones who have left my world for one reason or another. What about the two or three who abandoned me over the years without any explanation, or worse, who told me why to my face? Do any or all of these count as intimate relationships? Of course! Oh, my head hurts. And my heart hurts.*

5. **Losses where words fail.** Moberly states, "As always, these may vary by society."[37] These are all the losses when people do not know what to say or do. They may find it painful to face or discuss your loss. As Moberly states, "This only leads the griever to feel even more alone, misunderstood, abandoned, and without a sail in their grief journey."[38] This includes the following:

    a.   Check! ✓ *Okay, I don't have to mull this one over: the sudden, devastating, and unimaginable death, in March 1983, of my eleven-year-old cousin Dana, who lived with her older sister, Lisa, and their doting parents, Sharon and Eddie, in upstate New York. Dana had dark brown hair and lively brown eyes.*

She was athletic and vivacious. Sharon recently described Dana to me this way: "She excelled at every sport she tried; she was a natural. She was always smiling and friendly. Every teacher told us the same thing at our parent conferences—and they were not colluding with one another; it's just that they saw the same personality trait. They told us Dana loves to be first and she is very competitive, but when she gets to her goal, she turns around to see who needs her help. That has always helped us to know about her." Thus, as you can see, Dana was beloved by her family, friends, teachers, neighbors, and even the neighborhood shopkeepers and everyone else who was graced by knowing her, even for a brief moment. It has been many, many years, and Dana's parents understandably still grieve over the tragic and irreconcilable fact of her death. Sharon and Eddie's safe havens have included their grief therapists, grief groups, communities of other parents and families who have lost children, and those of us who understand and can hold and share the loss. And Dana's parents continue to honor Dana in all the social justice and compassionate work they have always done in the world and continue to do in her name.

Here is the double-whammy insult of disenfranchised grief in this case: Dana's parents also grieve over those close friends and family they have lost as a result of Dana's death, those same ones who did not know what to say or do. Perhaps they could not face the loss of Dana either, or confront the fears it aroused in their minds about their own children's mortality. Some of those friends and family disappeared from my cousins' lives forever. This is also a perfect example of the fourth key theme of disenfranchised grief above—the losses of relationships considered less significant than others. If Dana's parents talk about the pain and grief of losing these friendships, sometimes other people don't understand. "Compared to losing Dana?" they might say. "How can you even be bothered by those unthinking, uncaring bastards? They don't deserve your friendship. Forget about them!" Oy vey. They are trying to help, alas. But this is disenfranchised grief in its "perfect storm" constellation.

A special note: For Dana's family (myself included), for all her other loved ones, and for everyone who has ever lost a child or even more than one, I believe that the grieving process will never be finished, and the grief will never leave us. But neither will the love. Learning how to carry the grief and the love with the communion of chosen community and knowing the validity of all of it can provide solace. The never-ending love for and honoring of Dana and the light she shone on the world—and that of all the other lost children—will go on.

Moberly summarizes by stressing again: "There's one commonality we can underpin between each of the five themes. The causes of this kind of grief are all rooted in what society tells us to be true rather than what we know and feel to be true as individuals."[39]

Smitha Bhandari, MD
Board-Certified in Adult, Adolescent, and Child
Psychiatry from Emory University
One day during my research for this book, I found a fascinating 2024 WebMD article called "What to Know About Disenfranchised Grief." Smitha Bhandari, MD, medically reviewed this article. It concurs that disenfranchised grief is "when your grieving doesn't fit in with your larger society's attitude about dealing with death and loss. The lack of support you get during your grieving process can prolong emotional pain…even if you don't receive direct criticism from others, you can internalize the way in which you grieve."[40] *In other words,* I nod, *you internalize the grief, and you feel shame! Yup!*

The article cites societal attitudes and beliefs that echo those of Zoll and Moberly, which I have discussed at length. The four causes below, however, offer additional subtle emphasis and thus deserve mention:

1. **Workplace culture.** Some jobs involve experiencing intense loss. Emergency medical workers, doctors, therapists, and other professions can expose you to death and loss as part of the job. This can create a sense that these losses shouldn't bother you personally.

2. **Not a legitimate relationship.** Losing people or relationships besides spouses or immediate family members can still intensely impact you. Others may not understand why those other relationships are so important to you, which can make your grieving experience more isolating.

3. **Not showing the right emotions.** People have different emotional reactions to loss. Common images of grief might include crying, sadness, and depression. Some people react differently. They may show no emotion at all, feel relief, or another emotion others may not expect.

4. **Grieving a loss that isn't death.** The larger culture may frame [death] as the most important type of loss…some people may not understand why a loss affects you deeply if it's not a death.[41]

The article mentions nuanced, poignant, and so often disenfranchised grief situations such as the death of an abuser, an ex-partner, a patient, a pet, and the dementia or addiction of a loved one. I can hear the questions and comments that arise, even from inside my own head, and it makes my heart hurt. "Why would you grieve your abuser, or the ex-partner you parted from with such acrimonious feelings? They hurt you so much." Or "You are a doctor, after all; you see death all the time. You must remain professional and keep your emotions in check, or you won't be able to do your job properly." Or "You did not know that student…or teacher…or doctor well. They were *only* your student…or your teacher…or your doctor." *Yes*, I say. And if you *are* a doctor, a pastor, a police officer, a teacher, a social worker, or an elder caregiver like I was, society dictates that you *must* not dare show, express, or feel such deep grief.

These experts agree, and I agree with them. This is what disenfranchised grief looks like, and this is what can happen to us if we do not pay loving attention to our pain. But we are learning how to pay attention. We are learning that our pain, loss, sorrow, and grief do count, how to acknowledge it all, and release the shame that so often accompanies it. We *can* begin to heal. Let's learn more about how to do this in the following chapters. And then, get ready for some more stories.

CHAPTER ELEVEN

Our Society's Mandate Games for Grief and How the Wise Elephants See It

As Doka, Zoll, Moberly, Bhandari, and other experts attest, disenfranchised grief happens when one's society—as in our very own Western modern society—does not acknowledge, validate, honor, or support certain kinds of grief and grievers.

Doka's term *disenfranchised grief*, coined in 1989, speaks to this fact. Doka states the following: "The concept of disenfranchised grief recognizes that societies have sets of norms—in effect, 'grieving rules'— that attempt to specify who, when, where, how, how long, and for whom people should grieve."[42]

Because of these norms—these "grieving rules" for different types of grief, as Doka calls them—you and I and so many around us risk living with our brains and hearts washed in the fog of seeing such losses as insignificant. Society convinces us that we don't have the right to grieve; this becomes deeply ingrained in our psyches and wreaks havoc on our ability to grieve authentically.

As I have read, listened, and gleaned from these experts and pondered my personal and professional experiences living in this Eurocentric culture, I have come up with my own affectionate nickname for these grieving rules, these ingrained, unconscious, discounting, and harmful ways of thinking about life and grief. I call them our Western society's "mandate games for grief." As I see it, our society has created games we must play for constructing and conducting our daily lives, beliefs, and behaviors about everything! Society insists we must play by the rules to survive, to "fit in," to "do life right." In these dangerous games, nobody wins. For grief, such games can be literally life-threatening, and, as I mentioned, because they are so deeply ingrained in us, we hardly notice they are games at all, and we play blindly on.

Yet, there is some *good* news I have gleaned, some antidotes to our society's mandated grief games. I would like to introduce some helpful friends—the elephants in the room who never forget the truth about grief and grieving and want to remind us that it is okay to grieve whatever and however we need to. These wise, clever elephants hang out—often invisibly—in the rooms of our minds, our conversations, our emotions, and beliefs. Yet, they are standing right in front of us, crying out to be seen, trumpeting the truth, and hoping to help smash our false beliefs and our commitment to these mandated grief games into mangled, harmless heaps of detritus. They want us to remember that we need not play these games at all; we can see them for what they are, let go of them, and walk away. We can, with this simple knowledge, reframe, reimagine, and transform our beliefs and feelings about life and grief into, not pain-free, but shame-free, nurturing, and healing action.

Let us delve into these debilitating grief games to understand the havoc they can wreak, and then look at some antidotes.

1. The Black-and-White-Thinking Game
(aka the All-or-Nothing Game)

In our culture, this game demands that we must think of everything and everyone in terms of "black and white" (that is, "all or nothing," "good or bad," "success or failure," "win or lose," "smart or stupid," "right or wrong," "pretty or not pretty," "rich or poor," and on and on and on). I find "failure" a particularly sticky one because failure is *never, ever* considered to be acceptable or okay in our culture. Adding colonialist, patriarchal salt to the wounds, everything "good" is "white," and everything "bad" is "black."

In this game, there are no "both at the same time" positions that we are allowed to hold in our beliefs and our behavior. There are no gradations of feelings or colors or light in life—all is, at the most, shades of gray. There is no middle ground, and there is no "yes, and." In this game, we must search endlessly to achieve happiness and avoid pain.

There is no gold-medal winner; neither is there a silver or bronze. There is no winner at all; in fact, everyone loses.

The Black-and-White-Thinking Game dictates who, how, and what we grieve. When we grieve, we are either grieving "right" or grieving "wrong." We must be happy or sad, broken or healed. We are crying too much or not enough. Some grief is okay, and some grief is not. If we are grieving our husband of sixty years, that's okay (and even *that* grief has a time limit!), but if we're grieving our fifteen-year-old pooch who was so old and in pain anyway, perhaps not so much. After all, that old pet was just a pet. In this game, as stated above, we are all losers. We all know how it ends—in shame, denial, addiction, and suffering.

Our wise elephants remind us that the remedy for black-and-white thinking about grief is clear, but it is hard to remember without daily practice. The remedy is this: Black-and-white thinking *simply does not exist* when it comes to our feelings and beliefs and behaviors. The truth of grief is always nuanced, never simply one way or the other. The truth is everything in between the black and white. Grief is all those "both at the same time" feelings and positions, all the ground unfolding around us, all the shades of gray, and the entire rainbow of emotions in our hearts and bodies. Yes, grief is complicated, because that is what life is—and what grief—is. It is always "yes, and…" This fact can be scary; but it allows us, at the same time, to rest in a reassuring, albeit uncomfortable ease and acknowledgment of the limitlessness and impermanence of life. This way we are all winners.

2. The Five-Stages-of-Grief Game

This is Elisabeth Kübler-Ross's classic and (in my words) phantasmic and "must-do-in-the-proper-order-and-in-a-timely-fashion" game of the Five Stages of Grief. This is a variation on the Black-and-White-Thinking Game, and it has similar, sinister consequences for its players.

In this game, our society has created arbitrary and unrealistic timelines for all grief; it dictates that we should be moving in that smooth, linear, and lyrical fashion through Kübler-Ross's five stages of grief—denial, anger, bargaining, depression, and acceptance[43]—where we will eventually reach the fifth and final stage (but *do not forget* that important "must-do-in-a-timely-fashion" part!), when we'll cross grief's finish line, fall into the welcoming arms of acceptance and closure, and feel no more pain—ever. We are—or should be—"over it" by now. And if we are not, we are, again, not grieving "right." Our society's national anthem for grief is "It is time to move on…to get back to work…back to our normal lives. Our six-month…or six-week…or six-day…or two-day…bereavement leave (*gasp!*) is over."

As you may be aware, these five stages of grief have been used and misused, quoted and misquoted, and misrepresented and misinterpreted ever since Kübler-Ross first created, defined, and wrote about them in this now classic book rightfully titled *On Death and Dying: What the Dying Have to Teach Doctors, Nurses, Clergy & Their Own Families*, first published in 1969. The fact is that Kübler-Ross created the idea of "the five stages of *dying*" as a result of interviewing terminally ill patients to describe their many and varied experiences of the processes of dying, and to educate and support medical professionals and others who are supporting them in this process. She never intended them to be thought of as *stages of grief* that grievers *themselves* go through.

Dr. Ira Byock makes this clear in his passionate foreword to the 2014 anniversary edition of *On Death and Dying*: "Kübler-Ross famously delineated the 'stages' of denial and isolation, anger, bargaining, depression, and acceptance to meticulously describe the emotional states seriously ill people commonly experienced and the adaptive mechanisms they used to make sense of and live with incurable conditions."[44] Byock acknowledges this tendency for people, including scholars, to misconstrue her theory even when acknowledged for its original purpose. "Popularized as Kübler-Ross's 'stages of dying,' they have been criticized for suggesting a formulaic progression of phases through the dying process. Anyone reading the book will recognize this characterization as a simplistic and inaccurate representation of what she described. In *On Death and Dying*, Kübler-Ross made it clear that these emotional states and adaptive mechanisms occur in a variety of patterns."[45] *All right!* And there you have it!

And so, for grievers, even when using these stages as a general reference and guide for grieving, which can sometimes be helpful, it's important to realize they are *not* formulaic and they are not *stages*. When we cling rigidly to them, take them for gospel, and try to follow them literally, we end up only with more shame-laden, impossible-to-achieve tasks we must try to complete in the "right way." If we don't, we are grieving "pathologically" or grieving "wrong."

The fact is that grief simply does not work this way. As our wise elephant friends remind us, grief does not fit into universal timelines and stages. It is never linear and smooth. Grief is about phases, feelings, and way stations that are revisited over and over again. They can come and go, sometimes gradually and subtly, or sometimes collapse chaotically into one another. Anger and denial can flow into and around acceptance, wind through deep depression and despair, meet up with acceptance, or join up again with bargaining. We can have all our feelings and be in all these different places all at once for a minute, an hour, or a lifetime as we wander, climb, run, stumble, glide, crawl, and dance along the path of grief. Yes, grieving is like freestyle dancing; everyone's dance, their style, and their movements are unique. Learning to grieve is always messy, infinite, and ever-changing, just like dancing. Just like life. The path of grief is a sacred one and one to be honored.

3. The Comparison Game

Another variation on the Black-and-White-Thinking Game is the Comparison Game. Even when we are not thinking in terms of extreme and judgmental opposites, we still tend to compare ourselves to others, whether it is "*how* pretty or plain" we are, "*how* smart or stupid" we are, or "*how* rich or poor" we are compared to others. Here is where all the dismal shades of gray emerge. Again, the possibilities are endless.

With grief, we dwell on "how bad our grief is" in comparison to somebody else's. "Sure, my grief is bad, but not as bad as so-and-so's grief." As I have previously alluded to, this comparison game is one of the most subtle and elusive—yet insidious—ways that we disenfranchise our grief. When we compare our grief to someone else's with self-judgment and *at the expense of our own sorrow*, we make it less important, less valid, and less in need of attention. We shame it and dismiss it, and doing so can make us sick—literally sick in our bodies, minds, and spirits. In this scenario, when we deny ourselves the chance to heal, again, everybody loses.

Of course, we can be grateful for the comparative lightness of the griefs we might carry and for the memories, love, and joys we have had.

Having gratitude is as vitally important to healing from grief as the grieving itself. It is when we disavow our so-called "lighter griefs" and they become feelings we must discount and disown, that is when the harm is done. Amid our valid despair, we are thrust rudely back into the shame-riddled game of "not bad enough" to count.

The wise elephants bring us this antidote: They remind us that there is an alternative way of thinking about one's grief that frees us from the Comparison Game. Instead of comparing and discounting, we realize that there is no need for this. We can witness and care tenderly for one another as we grieve, and we can share this grief journey so that it does not have to be—and should not be—embarked on alone. We check in with one another; perhaps I can set my grief aside for a moment while we tenderly tend to yours, or you can set yours aside and be witness to mine. We can dive into one another's grief together, and, in this way, we support and lift one another up as we honor and carry these sacred wounds with us throughout our lives.

I agree with the elephants. This way of thinking (not a new idea, but so often forgotten), with all its intricate gradations of gray and all its inclusive "yes, and" statements, allows us to approach all grief and grieving from a place of acceptance and love. This gifts to us the profound, poignant, and healing balm that honors all grief, whether it is our own, that of our loved ones, our communities, or our world. Such inclusive thinking carries us into a place of camaraderie, connection, and compassion where we realize in a larger, deeper way, that it is all *our* grief—our shared grief.

Large, small, and everything in between, it is all valid.

4. The Blame Game and Its Antidote:
   Why and How to Forgive Our Unhelpful Trespassers
Here is a little flip-side view of the sufferer's disenfranchised grief where we turn our shame on others:

How callous and unfeeling of them not to know how bereft and devastated I am! How dare they? How can they ignore this?

Or, *How can they not say anything…say such a stupid thing…act like nothing has happened?*

Or, *They keep telling me how lucky I am it wasn't worse!*

Or, *How can they not have called me in months?*

Or, *Why do they call me every day and ask, "How are you feeling? Are you okay yet? What can I do to help? Nothing! Stop asking! Don't you understand that nothing can help?*

Like everything I discuss in this book, this is my point of view. I believe that when people discount or dismiss another's grief, or react in a stupid or clueless way, or do not react at all (even when they disappear from our lives entirely), we do not have to blame them ("blame" as in "judge them as being bad people"), and we can learn to forgive them eventually, if not sooner. When others discount our grief, it comes most often from people's misguided good intentions, their fears, their own unresolved and hidden griefs, or from its being too awful and simply not knowing what to say and do. Or, as is so often the case, it might be as simple as not knowing *that our grief exists at all* and that it needs attention! The reasons why some people do *not* acknowledge or support us in our grief are infinite, complex, and complicated; these reasons could fill another book on how we deal with grief, dying, and deaths of others in our society.

A note to those whom I have dared to call "unhelpful and clueless": As you read this, I hear the valid cries of protest going up. "Hey, that's me!" you say. "And, for your information, Rosie, no, I'm not clueless and horrible. I get it, and I want to help, and I'm doing my best! But I don't know what to do or say! Nothing I do—or think of doing—seems to help, or it's always the *wrong* thing, and I feel like a fool. And I'm scared! Help me!"

Okay, I hear you. And thanks for speaking up! I have some further reading for you, but for now, may this simple mantra be helpful to you: *Indeed, you cannot help.* By this I mean, of course, you cannot bring back that lost person or make that lost dream come true. And you cannot take away the pain. So, don't feel bad about that. The same goes for your feeling helpless.

What you *can* do to help is simply *to be present*. Being present in this case *is* simple, but not always easy. It can take infinite forms, practice, persistence, and a bit of courage. Let that person know you are there for them. Learn to be comfortable with *your* discomfort and grief. Yes—*your* grief and *your* feelings about what has happened and for that person who is grieving. And be willing to say the wrong thing. It's okay; you will do that. You can just say, "Sorry if that sounds ridiculous or stupid," or don't say anything at all, and then continue to be there. The important thing is, if this is a task you wish to sign on for, that you are present. Let the griever know you are there, that you care, and that you acknowledge and validate their pain. This can have a subtle but powerful effect of helping them acknowledge their grief if they are tending toward discounting it. And, if they are not ready to be seen, that's okay too. You can do as they ask, and still let them know you are there.

If they are open, you can ask, "What can I do?" They probably won't know. So you can make a specific suggestion: "Would it be helpful to you if I…?" Or, don't even ask. Just do it. (You can come and do the dishes, make the beds, or bring a meal—the worst they can do is refuse to let you in.) Or go out with them when they have to go shopping or to an appointment, or take their kids out. Anything. You will probably do and say the wrong things from time to time, but don't give up. You'll have plenty of time for do-overs. Just continue to let them know you are around for the long haul. And then do it. Be patient, be kind, and just be there in whatever form feels right to you.

The good news is that, in the greater scheme of things, there is nothing you can do wrong. The worst shit has already happened to them. Just be present with your love and support. They may not thank you now—or ever, but you will be doing what you feel is right in your heart for the person you care about.

***

Let it suffice for now to suggest that the neglect, mistreatment, or disenfranchising of our grief from friends, family, and even society is not usually meant to inflict more harm on the griever. Rather, from the micro (meaning our friend who does not speak of our pain) to the macro (our society's learned denial of grief and loss on a universal scale), it is more likely a matter of having succumbed to all those powerfully persuasive societal games discussed above. We don't know we can let them go. We have not realized, learned, and practiced—or remembered or carried down from long-ago generations—this alternative, ancient way of thinking: the inclusive way, the acknowledging way, the compassionate way to handle grief, loss, death, and the impermanence of all life.

We may choose to forgive others to bless them, but, as with all forgiveness, the most important reason to forgive is for ourselves. When we do this, we forgive ourselves, we stand up and walk out of the muddy dugout of the shame-and-blame game where "my grief is not okay" and "how dare they not understand!" into the light of compassion and acceptance of our grief and the grief of others. Thus, we allow and bless our wholeness and our right to grieve, thrive, and heal.

Caveat: If you never get to the "forgiving others" part, please do not worry; do not blame and shame yourself for *that* on top of the pain you already carry. Forgiving others is a goal, and sometimes, in this lifetime at least, it is simply unattainable, despite therapy, time, and all the other self-care tools available. Sometimes we simply cannot reach that goal. Please try to forgive yourself for that very unwillingness or inability to do so. You are only human.

5. The Olympic Games of Grief:
Having to Play All the Games All at Once Forever and Ever

This game is yet another variation on the same theme. It is all about "Something bad happened, but it's over now. We can go back to normal, just like things were before, just like it never happened at all." And so, we never learn. We all know how *this* game ends—the same way as all the others—in certain defeat for everyone.

This is the game where there *is* no final outcome; nothing changes, and we never grow wiser as people and as a society. I call this the most advanced-level, Olympic-style version of this game. And I believe it is the deadliest one of all—having to stay on the field forever, juggling every ball in every game at once. It's no wonder we become depleted, despairing, and numb. The defeat here is literally of Olympian proportions.

Stark examples of the effects of this game are the still-unfolding presence, fallout, and lessons not learned from the Covid pandemic. I believe that the pandemic should receive the "Olympic Gold Medal of Grief" in this most recent and ongoing society's mandate-games competition. I would like to share in its own section below how I unwittingly played the Pandemic Olympics and how deeply it affected me. I think it is that important. And I promise I will include the antidote.

The elephants are ready and eager to share.

***

My Pandemic

During the Covid pandemic, although I had my renters, we consciously crossed paths infrequently, and I spent most of my time in solitude at home. I had lots to do. I stayed up late, slept in, watched a million British murder mystery movies, and the twenty-four-hour news cycle. I read, I napped, I hung out in my pajamas, and I succumbed to the emerging adult coloring book craze. These were not "adult" as in X-rated, mind you. These were coloring books that were entrancing beginners and doodlers, experienced fine-art artists, and everyone in between. If people weren't writing a memoir, baking bread, knitting, or crocheting, they could be discovered busily and meditatively drawing all day and night in these books. The books contained endless, intricately detailed, black and white–outlined images just like paint-by-number drawings, but without the numbers. (Thus, you could use whatever colors you chose. What freedom! What a brilliant concept for Covid times.) There were big books, medium-size books, and mini-books, each with their own theme and filled with pages and pages of flowers, or mandalas, or cats, or country cottages—or busy Parisian streets, gothic castles, lions, tigers, dragons, unicorns, and even Seattle skylines. Instead of fat, clumsy crayons, the coloring tools of choice were high-end, finely sharpened drawing pencils with delectable names such as Custard Crème Yellow, Plum Purple, Sterling Silver, and Raspberry Rave. Megapacks of 364 pencils were especially popular. Drawing in these coloring books calmed me while I watched Netflix or listened to music or audiobooks. I never tried baking bread. That wasn't me. The coloring books engrossed me. I was hooked.

I wore my masks everywhere when I went out, of course. I had ordered multiple multicolored, multipatterned packages of cloth masks so I could at least be color-coordinated. (Keeping up with fashion trends was comforting, even during these strange times.) I wore my masks to the one grocery store I shopped at, and I ate lots of big salads, sandwiches, rotisserie chicken, and ice cream. (I've never been a prolific cook.) I talked, texted, FaceTimed, and Zoomed for meetings and with people I loved. I went for long, solitary walks in my neighborhood, and occasionally with my friend, Patrice, where we'd stick to opposite sides of the street from each other. I walked mostly when it was sunny, but sometimes even in brisk or drizzly weather. Walking in the cold and rain was a stretch for me, but I did it and was grateful.

When I walked alone, it was mostly leisurely. I listened to my audiobooks on my iPhone or took photos of the myriad flowers, birds, squirrels, and interesting front yards I passed. Some people were walking dogs or an occasional cat; others walked alone, too, or in small huddles of couples or families, appreciating the fresh air and the human contact while obeying the mandated six-feet-apart rule. I would nod at the other walkers. Almost everyone nodded in return. I could see the acknowledgment in their nods and sometimes the tenderness in their eyes, and I could sense their smiles behind their masks. Their eyes said, "We are all in this together."

So, I felt mostly content in my little bubble. At least, I thought I *should* be feeling content and fortunate. After all, I was getting unemployment checks from the state, I was not in danger of becoming homeless, and I did not get sick. I was lucky. I never did learn to bake bread, though—it just was not me. Despite all these blessings, I felt stunned, anxious, and sad. And then more and more anxious and sad, like most everyone I knew. After the first weeks, when it became clear that this virus was going to last longer than we thought or wished, these feelings began to pervade my senses constantly. After all, who knew if and when it would end, and what that might look like? I developed a niggling, repetitive thrum of fear in my bones, my chest, and my stomach. Bleak and violent end-of-the-world images began to show up in my dreams at night.

Soon, I began to plunge into comparison game thinking. With all my comforts and gratitude, I felt selfish for feeling bad. For me and my circumstances, there were perks. I was mostly relieved when it became suddenly acceptable to isolate—to be alone. I did not have to go out and socialize, or see anyone I would rather not see. And I did not have to maintain my vigilant presence on those intimidating, self-esteem–smothering online dating websites and keep those awkward meet-and-greet lunch engagements with two or three potential husbands a week. (Not that I had ever racked up that many dates in a week anyway—who was I kidding?) Here, finally, was the perfect excuse; it was Covid times. At least I was getting a much-deserved respite from that unrelenting, gnawing, but necessary life task. Thank God I could let go of that for now.

The more I read, watched, and listened to the news, learning about what was happening all over the world, the more I began to realize and understand my sadness and terror more deeply and universally. The pandemic was like an ongoing, slow-motion, haunting version of 9/11, with thousands of people dying, not just on one day in one city, but every day, day after day, all over the world. I found myself grieving in anticipation for myself and for what might still happen to me, to my friends and family, and my friends' families. And I was grieving all of it—for all the people everywhere; for people I did not know and would never know, who were ill and starving and dying; and for their devastated loved ones who could not be at their bedsides to touch them, be with them, and grieve for them in the usual ways.

I was grieving for the people who could no longer leave their homes to go to school or work or church, and for those who could not hug their neighbors or celebrate weddings, memorials, and high school and college graduations. I was grieving for the people who were losing their jobs and going hungry and losing their homes. I was grieving for EMTs, nurses, hospital custodians, doctors, meat plant workers, delivery people, teachers, childcare providers, and other essential workers who were being overwhelmed and traumatized—and dying, too. I was grieving for all the children who were losing parents and grandparents, as well as for the parents and grandparents losing children, babies, and grandchildren, and for everyone losing brothers, sisters, nephews, and aunties. I was grieving for friends losing friends, lovers, neighbors, and pets. It was for so many people losing so many others, as Covid unforgivingly and indiscriminately insinuated itself into everyone's lives. I was grieving with and for the whole world. That dawning awareness of what I would later come to understand as collective grief helped me to allow my grief to simply be. (See more on this in the next chapter.)

Then, just when I thought I had that all figured out, I saw that, as Covid seemed to finally be dissipating, somehow, somewhere, someone, or "someones"—in our country, at least, and in some other parts of the world—were chomping at the bit to be "back to normal," having decided that the pandemic was "officially over." There was no need to wear masks anymore, or to avoid large gatherings at conferences, weddings, funerals, or at church. Kids could go back to the classroom. It was as if our society was saying, "Okay, let's move right along; there's nothing to see here… let's open everything back up, go about our business, and go back to the way it was before." There was no need to make systemic changes in our society; no need to look anew at poverty, environmental degradation, social injustice, racism, or sexism; there was no need to revisit any of it at its roots. And, best of all, there was no need to grieve anymore.

"After all, Rosie, you did not die, and neither did anyone you know!" people said, including Blanche—especially Blanche. "Well, there was Kevin," they added. "Yes, he died, but he did not have Covid. And anyway, you didn't really know him that long." Ah, the arrow straight to the heart.

Got it, I thought as I held my head in my hands.

Here again, the wise elephants in the room raise their trunks and trumpet proudly: "Remember, Rosie! Just know that it was and is okay to grieve for yourself, for your own personal corner of the world, and for the whole world. It is okay—and important—and natural—and necessary—to grieve with and for everyone everywhere who is still suffering from the effects of the Covid pandemic."

***

In this chapter, we have learned a great deal about the nefarious and often deadly societal mandate games that deny us the opportunity to deal with life, grief, and grieving naturally. Fortunately, our benevolent elephant messengers have reminded us of what's important—that we simply *do not have to play*—we can *walk away!* It takes knowledge, lots of practice, and the courage and willingness to live with failure and uncertainty. This is how our shame dissipates, and how we can finally grieve without interference. Yes, these elephants are very wise.

So, I hope, dear reader, that by now you are starting to experience a bit of well-deserved relief, validation, and hope. For additional good news, let's look at the next chapter and see what else the experts have to say.

CHAPTER TWELVE

More Antidotes—
Further Words from the Experts

THANKFULLY, THE GRIEF EXPERTS do have more good news to share. There is new learning, new understanding, and increasing wisdom in our modern Western society and around the world about how to free ourselves from our debilitating, deadly beliefs and the games we play, including when it comes to grief. Partly as a result of the increasing worldwide sorrows surrounding us, such as the Covid pandemic, worsening climate change, genocidal violence, and more effects of "othering" and disenfranchisement on our species and our earth, we are learning to recognize, embrace, and tend to all these nuanced and infinite forms of grief. Only then can we embrace our promises to ourselves and our future. When we disparage, minimize, and disenfranchise our grief, we lose our humanity and we lose all hope of fulfilling these promises.

NIKKI MOBERLY, ICF, PCC, CBC
CERTIFIED MASTER END-OF-LIFE AND GRIEF COACH
In her article "Coping with Disenfranchised Grief," Nikki Moberly describes some new ways of understanding grief and disenfranchised grief in this world-encompassing context in a discussion of what she calls our "collective grief" as a result of the pandemic:

> In these past couple of years, we've collectively experienced new waves of grief and trauma. It's undeniable that loss of life due to the pandemic has led to incredible amounts of grief for millions of people around the

world….But we know millions have also experienced loss in social connections, predictability, normalcy, control, justice, and massive disruption to our well-being and mental health.

The American Psychological Association cites this collective sorrow, trauma, and anxiety as a result of the pandemic. This has led to this psychological crisis experienced by most—if not all—people living in this world.

Against this backdrop of this psychological crisis is collective trauma and grief. More importantly, this is a type of grief that society hasn't traditionally deemed as worthy of recognition.[46]

This description was another handy and helpful expert explanation of my own pandemic experience. *Vindicated again.*

Moberly continues:

In a time when the world is collectively experiencing an increase in grief and loss, it's imperative to support one another and recognize all grief as valid. Increasing our understanding of the different kinds of grief is more important than ever.

Without recognizing, acknowledging, and supporting all types of grief, we're disenfranchising ourselves, our loved ones, and all those around us who have suffered a significant loss.[47]

Yes, yes, and yes again. Amen.

FRANCIS WELLER, MFT
PSYCHOLOGIST, AUTHOR, AND SOUL ACTIVIST

If you read only one book on grief and disenfranchised grief (in addition to mine, of course!), I recommend *The Wild Edge of Sorrow: Rituals of Renewal and the Sacred Work of Grief*, by Francis Weller. Reading Weller's stunningly written book has brought me healing balm. Perusing *The Wild Edge of Sorrow* has opened my heart profoundly, compassionately, and self-compassionately to both the importance of honoring all our sorrows and nurturing hope. With care, humility, and poetic nuance, Weller has created the concept of all grief as fitting organically into his all-embracing "Five Gates of Grief." Weller wrote his book before the Covid pandemic, but he anticipates and tips his hat to what would become its fallout as he speaks eloquently of his Third Gate of Grief: the sorrows of the world, when "we register the losses of the world around us."[48] When I began reading this book, I thought, *This man understands disenfranchised grief, and how (in our culture, at least) all grief becomes disenfranchised at some point.* I was affirmed and grateful.

Weller's Five Gates of Grief are (1) everything we love, we will lose; (2) the places [within us] that have not known love; (3) the sorrows of the world; (4) what we expected and did not receive; and (5) ancestral grief.[49]

Weller's second and fifth gates of grief are particularly fitting in my case. The second gate of grief—the places that have not known love— are "the places within us that have been wrapped in shame and banished to the farthest shores of our lives."[50] These places, when acknowledged and honored and tended to, can heal. *Ah, shame again. Another standing ovation, please! Yup, that is certainly me…there are many places. My "ugly duckling period," complete with my budding, too-big breasts and my first menstruation at the age of eleven and a half. My loneliness, my depression, and my sexual feelings as a teenager. Yikes, especially my sexual feelings. All of them wrapped in shame! It's all about grief and claiming it. Ah, yes, that's what all that therapy has been about. Shedding the shame, healing the grief, and welcoming home my wholeness.*

Weller's fifth gate—ancestral grief—is the gate that beckons us gently into "the grief we carry in our bodies from sorrows experienced by our ancestors."[51] It knocked the ball out of the park for me. It confirmed what I already knew in my bones—and what still lives in my bones. It was ancestral grief. And it was mine. It had a specific name now, one that put it all into perspective and affirmed everything. My feminist, progressive Jewish social worker's mind embraced it all with tenderness, tears, and relief: *My Eastern European relatives came over from Russia, fleeing the pogroms, the killing, and the conscription. It was the story of Anne Frank and Elie Wiesel. It was the movie* Judgment at Nuremberg *I saw when I was eleven, and nobody talked to me about it before, during, or afterward. Why was I even allowed to go? There on the giant movie screen, measuring thirty feet high and sixty-five feet across, were the stark, black-and-white images of decimation, emaciated corpses, and mass graves, all so terrifying that I hid my eyes. There was footage of the German concentration camps and scenes of Nazi soldiers on the railroad platforms with their snarling attack dogs, running, yelling, wielding hoses, and spraying hard streams of cold water through the open barred windows of freight cars packed with bewildered, starving people of all ages. These were my people, my family, my history. These were the six million. This was my grief.*

Weller states in his introduction that one reason he wrote *The Wild Edge of Sorrow* was "to address the two primary sins of Western civilization: *amnesia and anesthesia*—we forget and we go numb. These two sins account for an amazing range of sorrows."[52] As I read on, I thought, *Wow, yes, this author is reading my mind. He is wrapping up all my thoughts in a bow of momentous realizations and confirmations. He is saying the same things I am trying to articulate! Much more eloquently, yes, but it's the same message:*

> I wrote this book for a number of reasons, most notably, to restore soul to grief work and grief to soul work. I feel grief has been colonized by the clinical world, taken hostage by diagnoses and pharmaceutical regimes. For the most part, grief is not a problem to be solved, not a condition to be medicated, but a deep encounter with an essential experience of being human. Grief becomes problematic when the conditions needed to help us work with grief are absent. For example, when we are forced to carry our sorrow in isolation, or when the time needed to fully metabolize the nutrients of a particular loss is denied, and we are pressured to return to "normal" too soon. We are told to "get on with it" and "get over it."[53]

…This "psychological moralism" places enormous pressure on us to always be improving, feeling good, and rising above our problems. Happiness has become the new mecca, and anything short of that often leaves us feeling that we have done something wrong or failed to live up to the acknowledged standard. This forces sorrow, pain, fear, weakness, and vulnerability into the underworld, where they fester and mutate into contorted expressions of themselves, often coated in a mantle of shame.[54]

…When our grief cannot be spoken, it falls into the shadow and re-arises in us as symptoms. So many of us are depressed, anxious, and lonely. We struggle with addictions and find ourselves moving at a breathless pace, trying to keep up with the machinery of culture.[55]

Ah, the shame, the mantle of shame.
Weller wants us to realize and remember this:

> We are designed to encounter this life with amazement and wonder….[56]
>
> …Grief work offers us a trail leading back to the vitality that is our birthright. When we fully honor our many losses, our lives become more fully able to embody the wild joy that aches to leap from our hearts into the shimmering world.[57]
>
> …Any loss, whether deeply personal or one of those that swirl around us in the wider world, calls us to full-heartedness, for that is the meaning of courage.[58]
>
> …In so doing, our hearts are ripened and made available for the great work of loving our lives and this astonishing world. It is an act of *soul activism*.[59]

To this, I say again, amen. Thank you, Francis.

David Kessler
Grief Specialist, Speaker, Author, Creator of Grief.com
Website and Podcasts

After Kevin died, I discovered David Kessler, his website, online podcasts, and his 2020 best-selling book *Finding Meaning: The Sixth Stage of Grief.* I felt like he was speaking directly to me about our society's mandate games for grief and how to step out of the fray and back into our lives.

In a webcast talk he gave on May 9, 2023, Kessler spoke eloquently about what I believe are those pretzel-twisting, gymnastic mind-game competitions we face when grieving our mothers. He stated that our culture often tries to fit even this so-often-complex grief into simple, one-size-fits-all boxes full of platitudes, and this foists shame on top of pain. He cited well-intentioned, yet deeply discounting comments that shame us for feeling what we feel. "She lived a long life. She was in such pain. She is in a better place now. You'll feel better soon, just wait and see!"[60] The variations are endless.

Kessler encourages us to claim all our grief, and to walk our grief journey in our own time and in our own way. He uses one of his favorite phrases, the need for grief literacy, below:

> …It is time for our society to become grief-literate….
> …We must learn to say "Your tears count"…
> …I see your pain…I may not know what it feels like for you, but I see it. I am here."[61]

He goes on:

> No one gets to shame you because of your grief, including you…if you are showing up one or two or ten or forty years later, I applaud your heroism…one's loss is [so often] unimaginable, although it may not appear to be so…and numbness and pain are its material. Honor yourself and honor your pain.[62]

Kessler offers us clear, indisputable truths about how the unsuspecting griever is hurled onto the playing field and into the frenzied, mud-spattered Olympian quagmire of grief-mandate games (remember those pretzel-twisting gymnastic moves I just described?). "So that's it. It's all over now. There's nothing more to see or do here. Just move along and get on with your life."

Kessler stresses how participating in such games imperils our ability to heal. He, along with these other grief experts, emphasizes the vital need to do something different by inviting us to honor, embrace, and tend to our grief.

Part III

***

Family Stories

CHAPTER THIRTEEN

Banished

THESE EXPERTS HAVE OFFERED us wise, hopeful, and even lyrical words about situations where grief is at some point—and sometimes forever—relegated to the dark and lonely confines of disenfranchisement. The discussions got me thinking more deeply about my mom and about the legacy of disenfranchised grief in my family, particularly ancestral grief—and the compelling word "banished" that Weller uses. Through this new lens, I'm learning how to acknowledge and honor all the fragmented, buried disenfranchised grief stories of my Jewish ancestors and myself along with the sweeter stories of Jewish life—study, tradition, celebration, community, faith, family, and joy. In this way, I can tenderly carry the enduring legacy of *tikkun olam* in my heart.

Thus, dear reader, I offer you a triptych of stories about my mom and me and our family—multifaceted, many-layered stories within stories of disenfranchised grief down through the years of the Wigutoff/Wigotow family. (Curious about the similar surnames? Read on; its relevance will become clear.) Before we begin, Romeo of Romeo and Juliet fame would like to say a few words. As you know, he had a very personal relationship with the concept of banishment.

Definition
Banish: (1) To require by authority to leave a country; (2) to drive out or remove from a home or place of usual resort or continuance.[63]

Romeo: "Rosie, when Friar Laurence told me that instead of being executed for killing Tybalt, I was to be banished from Verona, you may recall I said: "Ha, banishment? Be merciful, say '*death*,' for exile hath more terror in his look, much more than death."[64]

Clearly, Romeo considered banishment from his beloved Juliet a fate *worse* than death, while most everyone else in Verona insisted he'd be fine. He'd just never see her again. What could be so bad about banishment? This attitude, in my view, was a blatant denial of Romeo's devastation and pain and was, thus, a *clear* case of disenfranchised grief.

Me: "Thanks for sharing, Romeo."

Romeo: "No problem, Rosie."

***

Our first family story begins with young love, crescendos in the middle with not one but two cases of banishment with a capital B, and finally wraps up with a "happily-ever-after" ending.

My mother, Elizabeth Rose Wigotow, was born in Boulder, Colorado, on June 14, 1915, and my father, Benjamin "Norman" Wigutoff, was born on October 11 of the same year in Brooklyn, New York. They were the children of Polish-Russian-Jewish peasant immigrants, among the thousands forced to leave their lives behind to flee the starvation, religious persecution, and pogroms of Eastern Europe around the turn of the twentieth century (think *Fiddler on the Roof*, but much, much worse). Many arrived in America at Ellis Island in New York Harbor, and most never saw their families again.

Among those penniless and exhausted but hopeful people who passed through Ellis Island one day during that time were two young adult brothers, Ben and Hyman Vigotov. The family story goes that they went through two different processing lines, and as a result, they ended up with two different Americanized spellings of their last name. Thenceforth, Ben became Ben Wigotow, and Hyman was Hyman Wigutoff. Ben, my maternal grandfather, took a train west to Boulder, fell in love with that part of the country, and sent for his betrothed, Ida, in Russia. They settled there and raised their family, which included my mother, nicknamed Bessie Rose (later Bess), and her younger brother, George. Hyman Wigutoff, my paternal grandfather, settled in Brooklyn, found a wife too, and raised his family in the hectic, bustling, early twentieth-century New York metropolis. The family consisted of Hyman and his wife, another Ida; their first son, Norman (my dad); a second son, Al; and the sweet third and last child and the only girl, Sarah. Since you've been paying such close attention, you will have deciphered by now that Mom and Dad were first cousins, the children of those two brothers, Ben and Hyman.

It wasn't until 1934, in the middle of the Great Depression, when they were both nineteen years old and graduating high school, that Bess and Norm met at a cousin's wedding in Baltimore, Maryland. They were each the one chosen representative from their respective sides of the family to attend. It was literally impossible at that time for whole families to take time off and travel long distances. As the story goes, they "fell in love at first sight" at the wedding. Mom invited Dad—as any good cousin would amid the Great Depression—to drive out—I don't know if Norm drove or took a train or a bus—and stay with her and her parents in their little red-brick house in Boulder. Dad could become a resident of Colorado and attend the state college for free. If he stayed in Brooklyn, he would not have been able to afford college. So, he came. Of course he did. He was in love.

During the early part of the twentieth century, it was generally considered not a good idea for first cousins to marry due to fear of any offspring inheriting disease; in fact, in some states at that time, it was illegal. In the Jewish community, one had to be concerned about hemophilia, Tay-Sachs disease, and such. Thankfully, wedding one's first cousin was not illegal in Colorado, because Bess and Norm couldn't help it; their love was kismet. But Mom's mother, Ida, who had a keen sense of observation about such things, noticed that her daughter and Norm were likely harboring deeper-than-simply-cousinly feelings for each other, and she was not pleased.

Grandma Ida was not so much concerned about disease as a result of cousins marrying cousins. The fact was that over the years, she had become less than enamored with her husband, Ben. Although he was a proud immigrant to America, Ben continued to follow the "traditional old-world" style of husbanding and parenting—doling out daily spending money to the wife with rigid frugality and doling out punishment for the children's bad behavior with the leather belt strap. Ida worried that if my mother married Norman, she would end up similarly disappointed. Thus, for Ida, the thought of such a marital union was a nonstarter.

Bess and Norm, having equally keen senses of observation, could tell exactly what Grandma Ida was thinking and did not speak of their deep feelings for each other. But after a few weeks, when it became obvious that they were romantically inclined, the jig was up, and Grandma Ida took action. She made my father move out and forbade my mom to see him again—ever.

My parents were not deterred. They kept their relationship a secret for five long, lonely, and anxious years until my mother finished college and completed law school at the University of Colorado Boulder in 1939. Dad did go to college part-time and studied zoology, but never quite finished. For several of those five years, he was a teacher in a one-room schoolhouse in a small mountain town north of Boulder. He loved teaching there, and the rural remoteness of nature suited him, but he was sorely homesick for Bess.

In June of 1939, after Bess graduated, she and Norm decided to elope. They had no other good options. They drove to Denver and were married in front of a justice of the peace with their closest friends, Hugo and Helen Rodeck, standing beside them. Once the deed was done, Bess called her parents and sprang the news. It did not go over well. As this part of the story goes, before Bess had time to return home to pack her things, Ida threw her only daughter's belongings out onto the front lawn of that little red-brick house and vowed never to speak to her *and* her new husband—ever again!

As you can see, Grandma Ida, like Escalus, the Prince of Verona, who banished Romeo, had a tendency toward throwing people and things out of her house and banishing them from the loves of their lives for long, undefined periods of time. The problem was she had less mercy in mind.

Finally, one afternoon about a year later, Grandma Ida ran into Bess and Norm at a family gathering at a cousin's house. When she saw the adoring glances my parents cast at each other, Ida realized her error and decided to cease and desist. She could see she had been wrong about her daughter's handsome and devoted young husband; besides, she was pretty confident there would be gorgeous grandchildren to look forward to; and from that day on until the end of her life, Ida was Norm's staunchest ally and fan.

Again, according to family lore, it appears that for many, many years—and I can imagine maybe forever—Bess did not speak of her feelings about the first abrupt banishment of the love of her life, when Grandma Ida threw Norm out of the house; nor did she speak of the second banishment—equally abrupt, or more so—for her and Norm from her parents and brother after the couple eloped. The story of my parents' real-life love story became a well-known and oft-told tale about their fairy-tale "love at first sight," the thrilling challenge of secret courtship, elopement, and living happily ever after. It was a good story with a happy ending, and for my family, it was the only version that mattered. But it was not the whole story. There was never any room in this version for how traumatic these separations must surely have been for Bess and Norm, *and* for everyone else. Yes, for Grandma Ida, and Grandad too. Oy vey, poor, neglected, left out Grandad.

I believe that if Norm and Bess felt the slightest morsel of the pain that Juliet and Romeo endured when faced with the likelihood of never seeing each other again, then this somewhat more modern-day couple was surely devastated. I would declare that their banishments were banishments with capital Bs and thus grief with capital Gs. All the loss and grief got buried and became disenfranchised grief with a capital DG!

So, it went from Romeo's sixteenth-century Italy on into early twenty-first-century America. When we are left out of the sacred communal traditions that honor all loss, dying and death, our grief endures, unacknowledged and unresolved; our pain and our shame persist, and our sense of wholeness and belonging stay banished to the loneliest inner recesses of our minds and hearts.

CHAPTER FOURTEEN

Where Is Mommy?

THE YEAR WAS 1956, and the scene was the modest red-frame, ranch-style house in rural Annandale, Virginia, where I lived with Mom, Dad, and my older brother David. I was six, and David was nine. The story is about my first vivid childhood memory, which I have recently come to understand was an experience of disenfranchised grief.

That year, Grandma Ida (yes, the same Grandma Ida, who, only about seventeen years earlier, a year after my parents eloped, had become my dad's biggest fan and later became mine too) died suddenly of a heart attack while on a train traveling from Boulder to visit a cousin in Chicago. Grandma Ida still lived with my grandfather Ben in their little red-brick house in Boulder.

Ida was sixty-two years old when she died. My mom was forty-one. Mom flew the next day to Boulder to be with her father and brother, to help them with funeral arrangements, and to say good-bye to her mother. That was the first time Mom had ever been away from me, my dad, and my brother.

My early childhood had been typical of a "middle-of-the-American-middle-class" Jewish nuclear family in the 1950s, with a mom and a dad who had been married only to each other (and who, as far as I know, had never cheated on each other and were clearly still in love!) and the two requisite kids.

I was born on November 8, 1949, in Ketchikan, Alaska (a tiny Wild West–style fishing town on the southernmost tip of Revillagige-do Island on the Inside Passage, where there was a bar on every corner and where the women said about the men that "the odds were good but the goods were odd"). Dad was working for the Department of the Interior's US Fish and Wildlife Service as a foreign fisheries specialist, and Mom became the first city councilwoman because of her legal chops. We moved back to the East Coast when I was three and into our custom-built, modest ranch-style house. It was in a small, upwardly mobile, northern Virginia community just outside of Washington, DC, an area of tall pines and generous property lines where all the houses in this subdivision, aptly named Hillbrook, were individually designed and built among the natural forest landscape.

That first memory of when Mom went to Boulder remains vivid and terrifying in my mind. Occasionally still, when something happens to me that involves separation and real or perceived loss from an important person (or favorite furry critter), I feel that same sensation of existential terror crawling up through my insides. I feel like I can't breathe, as if I might die. It doesn't happen often these days—but occasionally, it still happens. Does that sound like a panic attack to you? I'm not sure. Maybe. But when people talk about traumatic separation anxiety, that rings all sorts of bells. I believe that was what I was feeling then.

I remember that I was holding the clunky, black rotary phone receiver to my ear with both hands as I stood next to its perch on the dresser next to my parents' double bed in their bedroom, and I heard my mother's disembodied voice crackling faintly through the phone line. My chest felt tight, my stomach churned, my body felt weightless, and I began having trouble breathing. While I could hear my mother's faint, faraway voice, I could not equate that voice with the person who was my mother. Where *was* she?

I don't remember what Mom said to me during that phone call— probably, "Hi, sweetie pie, I miss you. I'm fine." That was nice, but it didn't really help. My stomach continued to flip-flop, and my body felt lighter and lighter as if it were rising into the air like a balloon whose string some child had lost hold of. I could not touch my mother or see her. I could not find her anywhere. As far as I was concerned, as that six-year-old child, the mother who lived and breathed in my world was nowhere to be found.

In my brain, I knew that my mother had gone *somewhere* and that it had something to do with people "losing" their mothers, because after all, Mom had "lost" her mother, and now Mom was gone too. That was all I knew. And that was a bad thing. I don't know how long those feelings, thoughts, and sensations lasted. Was it seconds, minutes, hours, or days—or until Mom returned home to us? Or if they lingered even after her return—for days, weeks, months…years? Nor do I remember what life looked like over the months after she came home, but I guess things returned to what was called "normal," which meant I don't remember anyone ever talking about Mom's loss—at least definitely not to me, and again, not for many years.

I believe that this first-ever, full-color childhood memory, this experience of acute anxiety talking with my disembodied mom long-distance over the phone, was also my first introduction to disenfranchised grief. It was perhaps traumatic separation anxiety. (Is there such a thing as *nontraumatic* separation anxiety? I think not.) But I do know this: I cannot recall my mother ever sharing her grief with me over losing her mother, and that my fear and this anxiety episode during her absence went unattended. These facts fit neatly into our family pattern of disenfranchised grief, "grief that is not acknowledged and validated." Remember those earlier, never-tended to and never-resolved separation traumas between Mom and Dad, and between Mom and her mom? Ah, the generational gifts that keep on giving.

It sounds complicated, but it isn't really. We know now that grief that is never acknowledged, never validated, and never processed is never healed. No one talked to me when I was six, much less in a way appropriate for a six-year-old, about Mom's being gone or her grief over her mom's death. It was no one's fault that this did not happen; these were simply the kinds of things that people did not talk about in those days. And if there were whispers, they might have sounded like this: *Well, do you think Norma's okay? Yeah, sure, she's only six, after all. She probably doesn't realize what's happening. Kids don't understand about death at this age. I'm sure she'll be fine. It's life. Anyway, she's so mature for her age, I'm sure there's nothing to worry about.*

So, there you have it. *Of course,* I don't recall anyone asking me how I was when Mom was away! I was only six! And as bright and precocious as I most assuredly was, I did not think after that phone call to present myself to my father in my altered state of consciousness, tug on his shirtsleeve, and say, "Hey, Daddy, the funniest thing just happened to me. I think I just experienced a severe case of separation anxiety—which, because no one will ask me how I'm feeling, will likely remain buried and unattended deep in my psyche along with later events of disenfranchised grief, and this will affect me for the rest of my life. So, can I please have a hug?"

I was precocious, certainly, but not that precocious. Social work school was still almost two decades away, and it would be over forty *more* years before I was introduced to the term *disenfranchised grief.* But I surmise that a teeny-weeny acknowledgment of grief would have been a big help at the time.

Perhaps Dad—or any nearby adult on the scene whom I more or less trusted—might have said something like "How are you, sweetie pie? You must miss Mommy. She's fine, but it's okay to be sad. She'll be home soon."

That, and a big hug might have been enough.

CHAPTER FIFTEEN

The Broken Heart Syndrome—
Forgiving Mom

I HAVE MENTIONED EARLIER that Mom and Dad died only four months apart. They were both eighty-two years old. And yes, I grieved, but, as everyone said, often and repeatedly, they'd had a wonderful life together and had not suffered a day of truly poor health or lack of mobility. That was true. For years, my brother and I would occasionally discuss which of our parents would be better off dying first. The answer was always neither; it was impossible to imagine either one coping at all, much less well, without the other. So, those four months when Mom was alone without Dad after he died suddenly during what was supposed to be a four-day hospital stay for a routine medical procedure were ghastly. They had not been apart for usually more than a few days at a time since the day they had married sixty-three years before. Now she was not pleased. I understood. Mom and Dad were one of those forever couples.

Dad had been fine for his first couple of days in the hospital, but on the third day, a Friday, a massive stroke hit. The breathing machines were turned on, along with all the other beeping and zapping and humming contraptions that kept him alive and his vital signs monitored over the rest of that painfully long weekend, until my mother authorized the doctors to turn everything off so he could go peacefully. He did. It took less than three minutes.

By his bedside stood my mom; my brother, David, and his wife, Kathy; my dad's favorite nephew and niece-in-law, Eddie and Sharon (parents of Dana); and me. Mom was holding Dad's hands, but no one was standing right by his head, so without thinking, I took that spot. I stroked his forehead and told him he could go. At that instant—and I swear on a stack of Torahs[65] that what happened next is true—Dad's vacant, milky eyes, under his half-open lids, suddenly opened wide, and he stared straight at me, quite defiantly, I thought. Flashes of tiny, bright lightning bolts like something out of a Marvel comic book zapped out at me through those eyes. *Oh God, are you angry at me for telling you it's okay for you to go?* Or, maybe he was saying, "Jeez, thanks for the send-off, finally! It's about time. What have you guys been waiting for?" You know he was like that. He had mellowed, certainly, but the grouch still had its hard-fought residence inside. No one else seemed to notice this strange light phenomenon because no one reacted or said anything, so I didn't either. And then he was gone.

After all the obligatory signing of papers, making plans for the body, and the other necessary things that had to be attended to, Eddie and Sharon went back to their hotel to pack for New York, and David, Kathy, and I took Mom back to her house, where we were staying. We made our travel arrangements to go home, me to Seattle and David and Kathy to Prescott, Arizona. Mom had all her close friends nearby. She didn't say much, and she looked just about as blank as Dad did in his last hours. We were worried about her. So, David and I agreed that, once we were home, we would alternate calling her every night. We knew this was going to be hard.

It was. Mom suffered harrowing loneliness over the next four months. It tore at my heart to listen to her listless monotone on the phone. Over their long years together, Dad, always devoted to Mom, had indeed gradually mellowed into a genuine softie after retirement and was happiest as a house-husband, singing aloud to himself as he went about meeting Mom's every need. Dad managed their social engagements, accompanied Mom to her doctor appointments (as she did with him), and found great satisfaction in such tasks as cooking hearty, healthful meals for the two of them, even making her special, sweet-tasting strawberry morning smoothies packed with her vitamins. This was his true calling, and he loved it. Their life together had taken on the tender sweetness of love in later life. Think Ruth Bader Ginsburg and her doting husband, Martin.

Like most Ozzie-and-Harriet dads, when my brother and I were growing up, Dad dressed in conservative suits and ties and commuted thirty minutes five days a week to his office in Washington, DC. For twenty years, until he retired in 1974, he'd get up at 5:00 a.m. every weekday and have his first quiet cup of coffee alone in the kitchen with the newspaper, and then leave for the office about 6:30 a.m., before anyone else was awake. He was—unlike me—a morning person, and he enjoyed that solitary time. It was on those mornings, when every once in a while, I would wake early, sleepily pad down the hall and into the kitchen, and instead of Dad the grouch, I would find Dad the softie. He would look up from the paper, beckon me in for a hug, and say "Good morning, sweetie pie." I would lean in against his side, and, in those moments, it was just the two of us, together. Those moments, when I was a kid, were among the only times that I was not afraid of my grouchy dad's bark. In those moments, I felt safe in my softie daddy's arms.

Now, both the grouch and the softie were gone for good.

***

Every other day when I called her, I'd ask, "How are you feeling, Mom? What did you do today? Did you eat today? Did you get dressed today?" She had not been doing much of anything. I'd listen to her talk about nothing, and I could imagine what she was thinking: *Why are you asking me these stupid questions? You want me to actually feel my feelings? At my age? Is this supposed to help me feel better? Am I supposed to get over your father? Forget him? It's not like I'm going to find another husband!*

Well, I thought. *That makes sense.* It felt clear to me that Mom was making up her mind to go be with Dad. I knew she was not pleased at being abruptly separated again from the love of her life, this time forever—and, this time it really *was* forever. (This was even though my brother and I were still alive and thriving, at fifty-three and forty-nine years of age, respectively, mind you, and Mom took frequent opportunities over the years to remind us that we, her children, needed her supervision to live even minimally successful lives.)

Sure enough, a few days after Valentine's Day, four months after Dad died, Mom died too. It happened late in the evening of February

17. People said it was "broken heart syndrome." I looked it up; the literature says that broken heart syndrome can occur under stressful and emotionally upsetting circumstances, including after the death of a loved one or even as the result of a verbal altercation.[66] I was not surprised; not happy, but vindicated just the same. It sounded exactly right.

This is what happened.

Mom had had a weak heart after having rheumatic fever as a child, and she had developed a heart murmur. It did not present any problem for most of her life, but it became a concern once she was in her late seventies and early eighties. Now at eighty-two, she had been experiencing occasional acute episodes of racing heart and shortness of breath, and the doctors said fluid was building up around her heart. This was not good. Over the last couple years, it had resulted in a few scary emergency room visits—the kind that people love to talk about afterward once everything's okay again. Sometimes Dad would drive her, and sometimes she would end up going to the hospital in an ambulance. Dad would go with her in the ambulance holding her hand, so it wasn't as terrible as it could have been. Since I was in Seattle and she and Dad were in Sun City, I couldn't be there physically to support them. But she had Dad, of course, and David and Kathy were nearby in Prescott, Arizona, so I didn't feel too guilty.

After Dad died, Mom's cardiac episodes became more frequent. Out of nowhere, her heart would begin to race. She would feel sick, get scared, and call an ambulance, and they'd take her to the ER. Each time, the medics were kind and efficient, and each time, the ER docs were able to get her stabilized enough to send her home with confidence and instructions on how to cope.

A few days before she died, Mom had another heart incident. Like all the other times, she got scared, called 911, and was whisked off to the ER. Again, the medics were kind, efficient, and drop-dead gorgeous. I know this because she told me—she emphasized the drop-dead gorgeous part. However, this time her heart did not stabilize, and she was admitted from the ER to the hospital's cardiac intensive care unit. The doctor called my brother, and my brother called me, and I quickly made a plane reservation and flew down the next day. The doctor said that Mom's heart was not stabilizing as they had hoped it would, that it could take a while to do so, or that it might not stabilize at all. The message was clear: "We can't guarantee your mother's going to make it through this, so get your butts down here fast if you want to be sure to see her again while she's still alive."

My plane touched down in Phoenix early the next evening, and I took a cab straight from the airport to the hospital. Mom was awake, lucid, and in her usual cool-as-a-cucumber mood with a dab of annoyance-at-everything thrown in for good measure. David and Kathy were already there. Mom asked us to go the next day to check out the nearby almost-luxurious assisted-living facility (ALF), where several of her closest widow women friends were already comfortably ensconced. "I don't want to go home alone anymore to that house. I want to be where my friends are. And make sure it's affordable." Scrooge could not have said it better. We promised to do our best.

That night, David and Kathy drove us in their car back to Mom and Dad's house where we were staying. It felt surreal being there again so soon—without Dad, and now without Mom. Don't tell me that not all empty houses are spooky. They are.

The next day David, Kathy, and I went to see the facility Mom wanted us to visit, the one where her friends lived. It had the elegant name "The Heritage Regency"; like many a moderately upscale ALF, it sported a sumptuous, bustling lobby and sitting areas, a dining room, an impressive library, long hallways leading to residents' apartment units on the first floor, and elegant elevators and stairs to the upper floor units. A large gym and activity rooms were on a lower floor, and on the upper level, common areas were scattered with comfortable couches, tables, and chairs, and shelves lined the walls. The bookshelves overflowed with books, magazines, jigsaw puzzles, and games from Scrabble to Dominoes and Clue. On several floors there were activity rooms filled with arts, crafts, and music supplies. In the cozily arranged main lobby sitting area were numerous chairs and couches upholstered in colorful classic Southwest motifs. And there was a fireplace—yes, a fireplace, and, yes, it was always lit, even in the summer, although this was Arizona. Go figure. Anything for ambiance, I guess.

There was, in fact, only one studio unit available, which was what Mom wanted and what she could afford. It was on the first floor and cost (this was in the winter of 1998, mind you) $3,575 a month for approximately 450 square feet—maybe 500 if you counted the big closet. In addition to the closet, the unit consisted of one large room with an alcove-type sleeping area, a tiny galley kitchen, and a generously sized, handicapped-accessible bathroom complete with a tastefully tiled walk-in shower. A wide, spacious picture window looked out onto a well-tended garden of rock paths and sunny green cacti bursting with bright red and yellow flowers. The admissions director was, of course, gracious and honey-voiced, and she said she knew Mom would be happy living here in the same facility as her girlfriends. We put a twenty-four-hour hold on the studio and said we'd be in touch.

David, Kathy, and I had a quick lunch at one of Sun City's popular cafeteria-style restaurants—the chocolate cream pies were amazing—then rested a while at the house, and got back to the hospital later that day. Mom was sitting up in bed with her back propped up against a plumped-up pillow, working the *Sun City Daily Independent* crossword puzzle in pen. That was pure Mom—doing crossword puzzles in pen. She looked up at us and lifted her eyeglasses off her nose. We told her the monthly rent and the size of the unit we had found. She sighed, rolled her eyes, and looked disgruntled.

Wait! Was she having a seizure? No, the *disgruntled* part gave her away. It was simply that thing people do with their eyes—the *Merriam Webster's Collegiate Dictionary* calls eye-rolling "the action or gesture of turning the eyes upward as an expression of annoyance, exasperation, disbelief, etc.…"[67] Or, as Wikipedia adds, "a passive-aggressive response to an undesirable situation or person. The gesture is used to disagree or dismiss or express contempt for the targeted person without physical contact."[68] I love both of these definitions. Together, they described Mom perfectly. I didn't realize that she was referred to in so many reference books!

And, it made sense. Remember—she and Dad had been living in their comfy little 1,500-square-foot, two-bedroom, two-bath cottage with a landscaped Southwest-style front yard and backyard with a tile patio since 1974, when they had bought it for $28,000. It was one of the first little houses built for the fifty-five-plus retiree community in Sun City, Arizona, a city designed and constructed exclusively with folks like Mom and Dad in mind. As Sun City's creator and developer Del Webb put it in one of his original brochures: "Sun City Arizona Offers You America's Finest Retirement Living with Everything You Could Want...But at Costs Which Even Very Modest Incomes Can Afford."[69] It was true for Mom and Dad. They loved it—the dry heat, the constant sun, and the vast blue sky; the closeness to the Colorado relatives; the many amiable, active, and politically aligned friends they made over the years; and the multitude of art and leisure activities like silver and turquoise jewelry-making, square dancing, and movies. Dad had helped create the city's first synagogue building, and Mom played cello in the Sun City Symphony. (Dad was stage manager. You know how Dad always liked being close to Mom.) Best of all for their peace of mind and their own very modest income, they had paid off their mortgage years ago.

After her eye roll, Mom looked at us for a minute or so without speaking. Then she said something short and grumpy. I can't remember exactly what it was. Maybe it was "Okay, we'll see." That was it—the end of the discussion. And then she went back to her crossword puzzle.

We hung around. After a while, a nurse brought Mom's dinner on a tray. It was some bland, lumpy, hospital-food concoction that I could not recognize. There were also a roll and a bowl of chicken noodle soup. The soup was memorably salty because Mom insisted that I finish it after she declared she had had enough but didn't want it to go to waste. Do you know that "Mom" thing I keep mentioning? Do you get it now? I complied. I had to pick my battles.

But then she said something that was definitely *not* Mom. She said "Okay, you guys, why don't you go back to the house and get some rest now? It's getting dark, and I'm tired. I remember your granddad was really tired when George died." My Uncle George was Mom's younger brother, who had been born in 1916 and had died suddenly of a heart attack in 1972 at the age of fifty-five. I knew it must have been hard on Mom, losing her only brother who had been so close to her in age, and because of the devoted affection I knew they had for each other. But I could not recall her ever having talked about it with us. Her offhand comment shocked me. This was 1998. Mom was talking about grief—and grief from a time so many years ago. This was not like Mom, the ice queen. But then I did the math (and you know I'm not good at math!) and realized that Mom's dad, Ben, had died in 1960 *before* George died, *twelve whole years before* George. Was Mom just mixed up, or did she get it wrong on purpose? Was it too much for her to say, "*I* was the one who was exhausted by grief when my little brother died"? I'll never know; I did not correct her. Remember—I had to pick my battles. Again, we did as she asked, said goodnight, and went back to her place.

That night around eleven, I, too, was propped up in bed in my parents' guest bedroom, on the phone with my boyfriend Alan when we were interrupted by a telephone operator with an emergency call from the hospital. I told Alan I had to go. I heard a click, and a female voice came on the phone. She identified herself as a nurse from the CICU. She said that Mom had "suffered a major cardiac arrest" and had "just finished expiring." The words sounded so odd—so matter of fact—so routine. As if she were telling me that Mom had just finished having dinner. We needed to go back to the hospital. I hung up and screamed for my brother.

For a long time, Mom and Dad had had DNR instructions in their medical records in case of a life-threatening event like a severe heart attack or stroke. These instructions were in the medical chart that hung on the end of Mom's bed: *Do Not Resuscitate, Comfort Measures Only.* The medical team had honored her wishes. Mom had wanted to go be with Dad, and she had gotten her wish. Yup, I knew it. I was right.

So, it was true. Mom had gone to "the other side" to be with her sweetheart without a backward glance. Admittedly, I was peeved about that for a while. *What? Just like that? You're gone? You're done trying to ruin…ahem…run…ahem, ahem…be…a part of my life? Yup, just like that!*

But I soon began to get over it when the relief of not having Mom's chilling, judgmental voice in my ears and brain 24/7 every day of my life flooded over me in constant, surprising, buoyant waves. I was able to begin relaxing into my life in a way I never had. After the first few months of the "normal" acute guilt, anger, and regret-laden grief— normal for a middle-aged, middle-class, Jewish adult daughter dealing with the death of an aged mother who has "had a good life"—this phase began to lift a little. I stuck with therapy, of course. Getting to a place of relative peace would take additional years of hard work (and I believe firmly that this work, especially healing the most stubborn triggers from the deepest wounds, is never completely done. There are always triggers, as benign as they may become). That was in addition to what I'd already accomplished during the years before Mom died.

Yeah, I know, it's complicated. I do not miss Mom's go-to impassive weapon of choice when she was unhappy with us during those fractious teenage years—her icy look of love withdrawn. But over time, before and after her death, I began to learn how to forgive her. I know she did not mean to hurt me. It was that generational wound, the unfortunate gift that keeps on giving. And I continue to forgive her every day. It is a daily practice and a daily reminder—forgiving her and forgiving myself for not forgiving her. I loved Dad, and sometimes I sorely miss him. Not the scary, loud, angry dad from when I was a kid, but the occasional early morning, quiet moment–coffee dad—the mellowed-out softie who wore his heart on his sleeve in his later years. I loved Mom, too, but l don't miss her.

And just when you thought we were done with this sticky part of the story, I need to add one more twist to the tale. It is another common variation on the grief-mandate games I have not mentioned and that you might be familiar with. It's called "You can't miss what you never had." It's a *game*; it's not the truth. The truth is that I miss, I grieve, and I yearn every day for that delicious, albeit often fraught, mother-and-teenage-daughter bond I never had with Mom that I witness between some of my girlfriends and their now-adult daughters. It is also true that these bonds were mostly forged during a younger generation of mothers and daughters, and I'm deeply grateful to have created my own "soul kinship" relationships with some of those daughters and other young women I know and love.

Yet, I still grieve for that mom-and-daughter teenage-and-beyond relationship I did not have with my mom. We did not have the late-night talks complete with tearfully spilled teenage worries and confessions, or weekend mother-daughter getaways, or special woman-to-woman retreats in the later years. We just did not have that special closeness.

We were from that older generation—a generation of Eastern European immigrant mothers who fiercely loved, protected, and ruled—or tried to protect and rule—their daughters' lives. And yes, I know Mom loved me deeply, she did her best, she did what she knew, and I did and do love her, but I still do not miss her. It remains complicated—well, maybe not so much when you think about it—but it is still a daily work in progress.

***

So, dear reader, I appreciate you for hanging in there with me through this part of my story. This is a tough one, another complex concept, I know. But I am sure that since you have gotten this far in the book (and I thank you for that), you are at the graduate level of your crash course in understanding disenfranchised grief. I am confident you've got it. And, don't worry, there is so much more to learn and integrate, and plenty of time to do it. So, let me say a few more words about this last bit—grieving a relationship we have never had.

Each one of us has the need and the right to grieve the relationships we never had, the needs that were never met, and the futures we will never have or had perhaps for only a moment in time. Now this person, or part of ourselves, or our hopes and dreams, are gone for good, like the relationship with my mom that I never had and never would once she died. Perhaps your story is about a father who died before you were born, or a parent or another significant adult who, when you were young, abandoned you or surrendered you for adoption. Perhaps you had an emotionally distant or abusive parent or sibling, or a narcissistic lover or spouse or friend who could never love you in a healthy way. Perhaps you lost a newborn baby, had a stillborn baby or a miscarriage, or lost a child of any age whose future was then obliterated. Or perhaps there was a child who lived only in your hopes and dreams and was never conceived at all. Some losses may seem, and are, worse than others. But yours counts, too. It all counts.

The yearning for what never was and never will be—or for what was for that moment and never will be again—is valid. That trauma is real. And that grief is as real, as impactful, and as valid as any other grief. Yet this grief is so often invisible and thus easily ignored and denied by others and ourselves. This is the essence of disenfranchised grief. If we reject the grief and the grieving, we risk languishing instead of living. But when we can embrace our grief, and when we can acknowledge all our feelings and validate the yearning, the anger, the shame, the pain, and the love, we can begin to heal.

You know, the funny thing is that recently I have begun to think that maybe my mother missed our "never was and never would be" relationship, too. That gives me something new to ponder, and perhaps some new healing potential. It would not surprise me if you might have been way ahead of me on this one.

Part IV

***

Sadie's Story

CHAPTER SIXTEEN

A Different Heartstring—
Sadie Crosses over the Rainbow Bridge

THIS CHAPTER IS ABOUT another of life's never-ending love stories. It is about pet love and pet-loss grief. It is about the death of Sadie, my beloved Sadie Grace Wigutoff, the forever-petite, alpha-cat queen of my heart who crossed over the Rainbow Bridge (that's pet-lover-speak for when your pet dies) in the early evening of Saturday, July 15, 2023. My heart still hurts.

For context, I would like to share a bit more of my pet parent lineage alluded to earlier in this book. My first cat, Cruella, whom I adopted when she was just a rambunctious kitten, grew into a zaftig, round, and regal adult. She was a domestic longhair with light green eyes, soft-as-silk snow-white fur, and black markings. Her striking markings and her haughty but accommodating personality, along with an occasional surprise attack of bared but bloodless fangs, won her the name of Cruella de Vil, the wild, black-and-white–haired, evil heiress cartoon character with strikingly similar coloration from the 1961 Walt Disney animated film *One Hundred and One Dalmatians*.[70] She lived contentedly on grocery-store Friskies canned cat food and my devoted care for two decades, including moving with me from Washington, DC, to Boston and on to Seattle in 1987.

In 2007, when Cruella was twenty years old, it was her time. We were living on Capitol Hill at the time. She was ready to go but needed that bit of help, so I made the appointment with the vet. On the scheduled day, I took her in, and my kind and handsome young veterinarian, Dr. Ed Goodwin, euthanized her. I sat in a gray-cushioned chair in his office, holding her in my arms as he gave her the injection. Afterward,

I held her body for a long time. Dr. Goodwin said there was no hurry. How kind and empathetic he was.

Some three years later, after I had moved to North Seattle, I dropped into Dr. Goodwin's office on a whim to say hello and thank him for all the care he had given Cruella through her very last day. The receptionist gave me an odd look, raised her finger, and then, after a brief whispered conversation with another staff member, she turned back to me and said quietly that Dr. Goodwin had died of AIDS about a year before. I was stunned. He had been so young and so good to Cruella and me. It did not seem fair.

I told the receptionist what an amazing veterinarian he had been, how kind he had been to me, and that I was sorry to hear of his death. The receptionist was probably not supposed to talk to me further, but she was kind, and I looked so stricken that she must have taken pity on me. She shared that Dr. Goodwin's parents had chosen not to be involved with him after he became ill, and that his only sister took over and was there for him until the end. *Wow, what a gut punch.* The receptionist asked me if I wanted the sister's mailing address. I said yes, and the next day I sent the sister a note sharing what a loving doctor he had been. I cried while I wrote it.

My second feline child after Cruella (and my first adoption from the Seattle Humane Society) was Sweet Pea, Sadie's predecessor, who lived to be nineteen. Sweet Pea died peacefully in my arms at home early one Saturday morning after a gradual decline. I knew her time was near, so I had held her close all night in bed. She went quietly and peacefully at about 7:30 the next morning. At the time, I was fifty-seven.

***

About a year later, in December 2007, as you might recall, as soon as I returned home from Morelia, Mexico, and was safely ensconced back in my condo, I adopted Sadie from the same shelter where I had gotten Sweet Pea. Sadie was about two and a half years old at the time. Here is how that love story unfolded.

Sadie Grace was another stray, a petite, timid, long-haired tortoise-shell breed called a dilute tortie because her fur was a variegated color combination of muted gray, mocha, and beige, with a couple of white streaks on her face. She had been brought in by animal control after being found wandering in the upscale Medina neighborhood of Bellevue. She weighed about six pounds and had been fixed, but no one had come to claim her from the shelter within the thirty-day grace period that is allowed for such things. At the shelter, she had been named Sarah. I thought it wasn't too big a leap from Sarah to Sadie. At the time, I had a couple of human friends named Sarah, and the name Sadie was unusual and romantic. It reminded me of a name out of *Anne of Green Gables* or *Little Women*. So she became my Sadie. Sadie Grace Wigutoff.

Sadie was my perfect cat companion during all those years I have described as we lived our lives and encountered our many and varied human housemates and their critter children. She remained petite and mostly perky and content until the summer of 2023, just about two years after Kevin died. By then, she had begun to slow down—after all, according to one well-respected conversion calculation of cat to human years, she was about ninety-five years old by then. She was sleeping more, eating less, and moving more slowly. Her decline continued day by day, and by the middle of July, she was sleeping most of the time and a few days prior had stopped eating entirely. By Thursday evening, July 13, I noticed that she was trying to jump up onto my bed but couldn't do it. I lifted her up onto it and swaddled her in the warm bedclothes, and she seemed content to remain curled up there. Her eyes were closed and she seemed to be in a semiconscious, twilight sleep state, unaware of her surroundings and not in pain. She did not move from that spot again. It was clear that her body had begun its final move toward leaving the earth plane and me. Throughout that night I held her next to me in bed, and all day Friday I checked on her every few minutes. Again, that night and into the early hours of Saturday, I snuggled her against my body in bed.

I thought optimistically that her departure might be a smooth and easy one, like with Sweet Pea. I was ready for that. But later on Saturday afternoon, something happened that dashed my hopes and broke my heart. Sadie's tiny, still body began twitching uncontrollably for a few seconds, and then stopped. It happened again about ten minutes later, and then continued to happen every ten minutes or so. I held Sadie and soothed her, stroked her, and hoped for the best, but the twitching events continued. Thankfully, she did not appear to be conscious, in pain, or aware of any of this.

By the end of the first hour of this torture, I knew it was time to call for help. I put in a call to the emergency veterinary hospital, which luckily was only minutes away from my house, and I told the receptionist what was happening. She said I could bring Sadie in right away and there would be no wait. Sadie's eyes were still closed, and she was as limp as a rag as I lifted her into her cat carrier. She did not move or make a sound as I carried her down to the car and got the carrier buckled into the front passenger seat. A normal visit to the vet would have come complete with an enraged Sadie, shrieking and yowling, her fur standing up on end, and her legs stretched taut like four rigid spokes of a bicycle tire. But, this was no normal visit. As I drove to the vet hospital, I was already crying, repeating to myself over and over again, *No, no, no, no, no. It's not time. I'm not ready.*

When I carried Sadie through the door of the emergency hospital, the receptionist acknowledged us right away, and she had a technician take Sadie, still in her carrier, immediately into the back. As I handed her over, I could feel my arms go weak. I sat down in the reception area and filled out the obligatory paperwork. My tears had temporarily stopped.

In a few minutes that felt more like a century, I was ushered into the back hallway and an emergency veterinarian, a slim, handsome blonde woman in her mid-forties with a solemn, no-nonsense bearing approached me. We stood in the hallway, and I asked if I could see Sadie. She said yes, as soon as we finished talking. Then she led me through making "the decision." She had examined Sadie, and it was time. I knew it was time, but she said I had to tell them *in my own words* that I knew it. I had to say it. I had to say, "I want you to end her suffering." It was protocol.

So, I said it. "I want you to end her suffering." My mouth was dry. I did not want it to be true, and in my head I kept repeating *no no no*, but I said the words. The vet nodded and said quietly, "I agree with your decision." She left me for a moment and returned, carrying Sadie wrapped in a blanket. The vet handed Sadie to me, ushered us into an examining room, and left us briefly. I cradled Sadie in the blanket, close against my chest.

The vet returned, much too quickly this time, with the injection syringe. I laid Sadie gently on the examining table on top of the blanket. I noticed it was a soft, muted gray-and-burgundy wool with a traditional, intricate Kalamkari Indian pattern. I know this because I remembered later to look it up online, the memory of it was so vivid. *It was beautiful, elegant, and unique,* I thought, *so fitting for my beautiful, elegant Sadie.* I laid my hands on her while the doctor gave her the shot. It took less than a second for Sadie's mouth to go rigid. I asked the doctor if I could listen through the stethoscope she was holding against Sadie's side. The doctor said yes and handed it to me. I put the earpieces in my ears and listened, but I heard nothing, only black emptiness. She was gone, so quickly. "You're the only person who's ever asked to do that," the vet said softly, in a tone I thought sounded admiring.

The doctor left us and I did not see her again. I picked Sadie up and sat holding her body to my chest again, rocking her and talking to her until a nurse brought in more paperwork. The nurse said I could stay with her until I was ready. *I will never be ready.* The tears began again. A few minutes later, I called the nurse back in and let her take Sadie out of my arms and carry her out of the room. That hurt the most, the act of placing my feline child's inert body into a stranger's arms—and watching that stranger take her away from me forever. And then came the part that hurt even more: walking out of the little building carrying Sadie's empty cat carrier. It felt so light.

***

A few nights later, I called my friend Barb to let her know that Sadie had died. Barb loved Sadie. They had met over the years and Barb was Sadie's official "cat auntie." Barb loves to send greeting cards and note cards the old-fashioned way: written by hand, sealed in an envelope with a first-class stamp, and set out in the mailbox with the red metal flag on the side of the mailbox flipped up. She would send me "Happy Birthday" cards from Sadie and "Happy Mother's Day" cards too, always signed "To Mom, from Sadie," and with phrases like "Barb helped me pick out this card for you, she helped me with my penmanship, and she helped me seal the envelope. You are the best mom ever. Love, Sadie." It was a hoot.

That night, on the phone, Barb said, "I'm so sorry, Rosie. She was such a good kitty. Yes, it's a love relationship of its own kind, with a creature who depends on you and loves you always. It's different, but it is still love, and we still grieve. It pulls a different heartstring."

Yes. In that moment, I knew Sadie would be the heroine of this chapter, and I would title it "A Different Heartstring." It says it all.

"It's so good to have people in our lives who get it. Thank you, Barb," I said, with a lump in my throat.

***

The package I received from Timberline Emergency Hospital about ten days after Sadie died contained a carefully wrapped clay imprint of her paw and a pet-loss grief brochure. The clay paw imprint freaked me out a little, because I could tell it was hers. But I was impressed with the brochure. It said that, like any grief, like *all* grief, when you lose a pet, you feel the loss, and you can feel literally "lost." I get it. That's how I'd been feeling in those first days, just like when Kevin died. That's how I had felt after each of my previous cat companions had died. And, yes, with my parents, too.

One thing the pet-loss grief brochure did *not* state outright was the fact that—as you, my dear reader, know by now and very likely from personal experience—pet-loss grief is a significant type of disenfranchised grief in our society. Simply being armed with that knowledge could free so many grieving pet parents at least of the shame that forces them to grieve in secret or bury their pain and sorrow completely. I thought I might contact the pet brochure people one of these days and have a little chat with them about that. To its credit, the entire brochure validated that pet-loss grief *is* real, simply by its very existence and the fact that it was sent to the grieving people left behind. After all, it *was* titled *Coping with the Loss of a Companion Animal: Support Guide for Families.*[71]

It's a fact. We can grieve for our furry or feathered or scaly children just as we grieve for our human loved ones. The brochure also said that, like with all grief, we humans can always find some reason to feel guilty about how it went down. That is so true. Even though I'd been the best cat mom ever to Sadie, in those first days after she died, I experienced gut-wrenching guilt. *Oy vey, yes. I could have done something to prolong her life. I could have taken her to the ER sooner. I didn't soothe her enough in that last half hour as I sat holding her in my arms in the exam room at the emergency veterinary hospital, waiting for the vet to bring in the "forever sleep" injection.*

I did soothe her, though, in those last moments in that room in the emergency clinic. I held her close and rocked her, her light-as-air little body against my chest. I talked to her, cried, kissed her head, and told her over and over what a good girl she had been and that I loved her so much. I buried my face in her fur, so I could feel the softness of her one last time. And then, I let her go.

In those days after Sadie died, I was learning even more through my exploration into disenfranchised grief how the guilt and shame over my grief could be embraced, acknowledged, and laid to rest so I could hold that grief for my girl lovingly in memory and celebration of our long years together.

Below are a few bits from my journal in the weeks after Sadie died. They might make you cry a little or even a lot; you need not be surprised or alarmed. Your feelings are normal; it's part of grief. You need not feel ashamed or guilty, but, if you do, know that is part of real grief, too. It's okay to feel it and let it go.

July 26, 2023
Letter to Sadie: *Hi, Sadie, my sweet, most fair, and beautiful kitty in the whole world. Like I used to tell you a hundred times a day, I love you. I hope you are okay. I hope you saw the hummingbird come to greet me this morning on the deck. Mom*

Reply: *Dear Mom, thanks for being such a good mom. We had a great life together. Thanks for holding me so close at the end. I wasn't scared. I love you, and I am okay. And I saw the hummingbird encounter. I was there. And I'm here. Goodnight.*

July 29, 2023
It has been about two weeks since Sadie died. All day long, I feel mini-zaps, sharp, quick electric shocks that surge briefly through my chest and stomach. It happens when I'm standing in the kitchen, or sitting in the

living room, or wherever I happen to be in the condo. I keep turning my body automatically, expecting to see Sadie emerging from the bedroom, or jumping down from her favorite perch on the living room windowsill to come join me, bumping her head against my outstretched hand, or rubbing her body against my legs, sometimes starting to yammer for breakfast or dinner. Or, as I'm carrying my laundry basket into the living room, heaped full of freshly laundered and invitingly warm dry clothes, I think I can see her scampering along beside me until I set down the basket, and she leaps into the pile of clothes inside, burrows down like a mole, disappears under the warm towels and jeans and undies, and remains there for hours. By then, the clothes would not be warm anymore, but she was often still there, peeking out at me, her green eyes lazily opening and closing. Now she's not there. She's not anywhere.

I don't feel the acute grief as much during the day when I'm busy with my life. I am not sure why. Sadie and I were here in this condo together every day for the past fifteen years, except for a couple of days or weeks here and there when I was working overnight or away on vacation. Every night at bedtime, as soon as I laid my own body down in bed, she would join me, lying on my chest with her perfect soft nose bumping up against mine, her paws under her chest, or curled on her side next to me spoon-fashion inside the crook of my outstretched arm or pressed against my stomach.

August 2, 2023

Sadie is still gone. That is the trouble with time passing. The ache gets worse as it becomes clearer that she's gone for good. Now I look for her less throughout the day, but when I do, my belly aches with a stab of sadness, and the missing comes like a quick punch in the gut. Then the ache rises into my chest, settles in my heart, and remains there until my attention gets focused at some point on other things, and the ache dissipates.

Funny thing. I met a nice man today.

August 23, 2023

Tonight, I opened a can of chunk-light, low-sodium tuna fish in water for the first time since Sadie died. That quick jolt of pain rose. It was the first time in fifteen years that I heard no skittering, of eager little cat feet as Sadie would jump down from wherever she'd been napping or perching or grooming, and careen around the corner of the bedroom like a miniature race car driver and into the kitchen to begin her high-pitched, squalling siren song of "Tuna-fish, tuna-fish, tuna-fish juice, pleeassse!" It was our ritual. Tuna fish for me and the juice for her.

I pressed the can opener into the rim of the can, turned the handle, and then, not thinking, with the lid, I squeezed the tuna juice into a bowl. Then it dawned on me. There would be no wrestling match as I set down the bowl before it spilled because there was no frantic, furry, eager head butting against my hands, no body wriggling between my legs, and no face pushing into the bowl and lapping up the juice. None of that happened. I felt the gut punch, the sadness, the yearning. I sighed. I had no use for the tuna fish juice. I poured it down the sink drain. Then I got the mayo out of the fridge and made myself a tuna fish sandwich.

The man I met is sad for me. He's sweet. His name is Michael.

***

At present, my never-ending story of pet love is in its most recent bitter-sweet intermission. I may adopt again once I take a break, and perhaps get some more travel fever out of my system. It will definitely be a senior critter, so we can share our twilight years together! Who knows? It might even be a little dog. A cuddly one.

CHAPTER SEVENTEEN

For the Love of Pets— a New Friend

A FEW WEEKS AFTER the tuna-fish juice incident, I was deep into writing my grief memoir and was becoming moderately wiser in the ways of disenfranchised grief. So, I was not surprised when, in the bathroom late one night, I was scrolling through YouTube on my iPhone during my nightly toothbrushing ritual and came across a 2022 TEDx Talk by Dr. Sarah Hoggan, DVM, titled "Pet Loss Grief: The Pain Explained."[72] *Okay*, I thought. *This sounds pertinent. And this Dr. Hoggan looks like a nice person.* I stopped scrolling, turned off the electric toothbrush, leaned against the edge of the sink counter, and watched the whole video. I listened, and my tears came. The talk was sixteen minutes and forty seconds long. Not that long but long enough to say it all. It *was* pertinent, of course—more than I could have imagined. I listened a bunch of times that night and in the days to follow. And I took notes.

In the talk, Dr. Hoggan discusses how devastating it is for so many of us when we must euthanize a pet. Distraught pet parents start to cry in her office, and some immediately start apologizing. She tells them,

> You don't have to apologize to me. This is what I have dedicated my life to.…The pain of pet loss is real because the emotions you shared with your pet were real. The grief associated with pet loss is valid because you didn't lose a thing. You lost a *someone*—someone close and someone special to you.[73]

Yes, yes, of course, I thought. *That's always been the way with me and my kitties.*

Dr. Hoggan went on to explain *how* the pain of losing a pet is valid and unique from losing a human:

> It is different for multiple reasons. The first reason is that our society tends to diminish the validity of the pain of pet loss. They act like it is almost histrionic. *Histrionic* is a word that means theatrical, like you're just grieving for attention.[74]

Ah, there it is! Diminishing the validity of our loss! Acting like it's silly and frivolous! Damn. That's disenfranchised grief. Good grief. And she's confirming that, yes, this is that different and sacred heartstring that's getting pulled.

After I listened all the way through, I backed up the video and ran for a pencil and paper. Then I scribbled notes as I listened again and then again. She continued:

> Nobody questions our pets' ability to make us happy.… If our pets can make us so happy that we laugh out loud, then losing them can absolutely have the opposite effect and break our heart.[75]

Oh, my heart. Okay, Sadie. I need to speak with this person. This is so timely and perfect and important for the book. The next day, I left a message at the VCA California Veterinary Specialists in Murrieta, California, where Dr. Hoggan was the medical director and veterinary emergency physician, where she oversaw emergency and critical care services, and where, as she says in her talk, she was intimately involved every day with having to euthanize beloved critters and be with their grieving pet parents.

I explained to the receptionist on the phone that I was writing a memoir about disenfranchised grief and that I recently had to have my own cat Sadie euthanized. I told her I had just watched Dr. Hoggan's TEDx Talk about the crushing reality of pet-loss grief and society's discounting of it; her talk spoke to a kind of disenfranchised grief that I was discussing in the book, and it had resonated deeply. I hoped Dr. Hoggan would contact me so we could chat a bit.

"Absolutely," the receptionist said. I left my phone number. The next day, Dr. Hoggan texted me. I texted back that same day, and we made a plan to talk on the phone.

When I heard Dr. Hoggan's warm, embracing voice on the phone, that same voice I had heard on her TEDx Talk, I felt as if I had rediscovered an old friend. I grabbed my pencil and paper. We talked about Sadie, about all the dogs and cats who live with Dr. Hoggan and her boyfriend (now husband), and about her long and dedicated career as an emergency animal-hospital veterinarian. Dr. Hoggan said that, yes, in her practice, she sees the issue of disenfranchised pet-loss grief constantly; she encourages families to allow themselves to grieve and to begin to think of euthanasia as the kindness it is.

Dr. Hoggan told me that, as successful as she may be in supporting these bereaved families, the fact remains that among the veterinary medical and support staff themselves, their grief at being involved in and exposed to such constant loss and death, including euthanasia, typically goes unnoticed and unappreciated. Thus, their grief becomes disenfranchised as well. This disenfranchised grief, Dr. Hoggan believes, is one often-recognized reason why veterinary professionals, especially veterinary emergency-room professionals, have among the highest rates of suicide in the United States. In response to this frightening statistic, she said, the organization called Not One More Vet was created in 2014. The NOMV website says, "NOMV's mission is to transform the status of mental wellness within the profession so veterinary professionals can survive and thrive through education, resources, and support."[76]

This stunned me, and I was grateful to learn about NOMV. I had no idea. I had never thought of disenfranchised pet-loss grief for all those veterinary folks. Dr. Hoggan told me how grateful she is that NOMV exists and is providing much-needed support and tools for emergency and all veterinary professionals. Her clinic also has a full-time therapist on staff to provide support to all employees, and she has her own therapist, too, who supports and encourages her to feel her grief for her pet patients and their families and to "feel all her emotions," including in all areas of her life where grief resides.

Thus, Dr. Hoggan passionately advocates tending to the often-disenfranchised grief of pet loss; she believes a self-forgiveness-over-time process must be available for pet-loss grievers so that they can bring their pain into the light, honor their grief, and ease their shame over it.

Dr. Hoggan agreed with me about being able to contemplate forgiving those "clueless ones" (her words), meaning those who "don't get" pet-loss grief and discount it. Her laugh was sympathetic when I used *my* words to describe such folks as those "unhelpful people." By learning to understand and forgive them, we grievers can be freer from our own disenfranchised grief and shame, because we understand that it is hard for people to validate such grief in anyone, including themselves. She believes from her experience that those who "do not get it" have simply never experienced pet love. Or, they *have* experienced the love and loss of a pet at some point, only to have *their* loss—*and* their love—dismissed and disenfranchised. So, their grief has also had to be buried and denied.

No matter what the reason, Dr. Hoggan emphasized, these folks "are not being unhelpful on purpose, and are as worthy of compassion and understanding as anyone else." (Be reassured, dear reader, that this kind of forgiveness is a goal and can take time, and sometimes we just can't do it, and that is perfectly fine. I have already spoken a bit in Chapter Eleven about the goal of forgiving ourselves when forgiving others turns out to be just too much. We have enough on our plates without having to feel bad about that!)

Finally, Dr. Hoggan emphasized that allowing one's grief over the loss of a pet can support their efforts to "love another deserving animal" after a period of natural mourning time. Sometimes, just as in human relationships, denying the validity of one's grief over a pet compels people to deny themselves for too long—sometimes forever—the opportunity to love another furry or scaly or feathered critter: *No, I can't get another pet yet. It's too soon. It still hurts too much. It would be disloyal, a betrayal.*

And feeling that way is okay. Each person has their own grief timetable for pets as well as everything else. And sometimes the grief *is* too much, and it is okay to say "no more," even forever. But hopefully, the permission to allow and heal one's grief over a beloved pet will open the door for more humans to reach out to the next deserving critter. Because they *do* deserve your love. And you deserve *their* love.

As we finished up, Dr. Hoggan asked if I would text her a few photos of my gorgeous Sadie. Then Dr. Sarah—by this point in the phone conversation, we were on a professional first-name basis—told me to stay in touch about my book, and she invited me to visit her and her furry family menagerie in California anytime.

After our call, I knew that I had found another expert voice who cares passionately about this urgent, literally life-and-death message— the need to educate people about honoring their pet-loss grief.

***

In sum, pet-loss grief is unique, yet it can be as painful as the grief we feel for our humans. We feel that unconditional love our pets bestow upon us, we love them back, and we feel that loss deeply. Our critters do pull on a different heartstring within us—an equally sacred one. We feel the loss, the emptiness, the anger, and the depression. We feel the ache, the yearning, and the missing. We might feel guilt—*I should have—or could have—done something differently. I could have—or should have—been a better pet parent.* Yes, we can feel shame over our actions and if we grieve "too much." Yet, the fact is that our grief over our animal children is valid; all of our feelings about losing our pets are normal and deserve our self-compassion, attention, and care.

Some days after my phone conversation with Dr. Sarah, as I continued to write about pet-loss grief, I found myself thinking again of Mom and her not knowing how or having permission to grieve openly and heal from so many of the profound losses in her life. It occurred to me to wonder if the same was true for her about pet-loss grief. I was only about two years old, too young to remember this firsthand, but I recall hearing in later years a few of the remarks Mom had made when our family's aged little yellow mutt, Susie, died. I don't remember Susie, but I know she was the only dog my parents had during those early years of marriage and would ever have. When Susie died, Mom had said something like, "I never want another pet in this house. I will not have it. They are just too much work, and they make too much of a mess."

Does that sound like a case of buried grief to you? Maybe or maybe not. Maybe Mom just didn't like dogs. They *are* a lot of work, and they *do* make messes. But knowing her, I'd venture to say it was disenfranchised grief. I know the pain of loss was rough on her. According to people who knew her, she did not say, "Another pet will eventually die too, and I could not bear it again." (You know Mom wasn't much for talking about painful feelings.) If she *had* said something, once I was old enough, I might have understood her wish to avoid facing that kind of grief again.

Instead, forever after that, our family was a home, perhaps with a little less grief in it, but also with less love, the unique love of a cherished pet.

CHAPTER EIGHTEEN

Inside the Road Map—
Things to Do Along the Way

So, DEAR READER, we have been using this book—the self-compassionate road map I spoke about in my introduction—on our journey to learn how to identify, acknowledge, engage with, and reenfranchise our disenfranchised grief. This final chapter contains your handy glove compartment "road map insert" containing activities and exercises, bits of wisdom, anecdotes, gentle reminders, tips, and ideas on how to be present with your grief in healthful, constructive, contemplative, soul-engrossing, and even playful ways. You can dip into them, hang out with them, and use them whenever the mood strikes and as you wish.

These ideas are presented in no particular order and are not an exhaustive compilation; they are simply meant to get your mind percolating and to help you reflect, learn, feel, cry, heal, have fun, and enjoy the ride.

You can copy or take screenshots of these pages, print them out, and staple them together for easy access, or use a three-hole puncher and insert them into a colorful binder. Or keep them handy and use them as a jumping-off point for doing your own thing!

***

Things to Read and Contemplate
(including Rosie Wisdom, Wise Quotes, and Anonymous Quotes)
These are familiar sayings and quotes that I appreciate. Some of them I have created myself (and humbly named "Rosie Wisdom"). A couple I have heard, loved, and absorbed over the years without knowing their origins, or they are anonymous, and thus I have no attributable sources for them. Most others are quotes from wise people wherein I was able to find citations. The citations assist you in exploring these authors further if you are intrigued.

More Things to Read and Contemplate—Anecdotes
These are story snippets from people who talked with me while I was researching and writing this book, along with a few of my own.

Things to Write and Contemplate
These are writing and contemplation exercises that include journaling, responding to grief prompts, list-making, variations on the theme of gratitude journaling, and, last but not least, Rosie's LAVIE Method (I love French!).

Things to Do—Action Steps
These are suggestions for ongoing and future action, such as meditation and therapy.

Things to Do for Fun
These are a bunch of fun, silly, and engrossing activities to dip your toes into one toe at a time, or wade in up to your knees, or jump right into head- or feet-first.

Final Reminders for the Road
These include vital items such as packing snacks. They *are* vital. Remember them.

So, buckle up, and let's get on the road!

Rosie Wisdom
Grieve is an action word.
Life involves being in continual grief processes,
sometimes many at the same time.

As we allow ourselves to grieve, we become more humble, grateful, joyful,
and committed to doing our best and being our best selves—
for those we have lost, for the ones we still have, and for ourselves.

Grieving is a form of self-care, of communion and connection
with others, and a form of caring for others in grief
that allows theirs and ours to be borne.

Anecdote: My First True Doggie Love Affair

My old boyfriend Chet's sweet old mutt, Buddy, had the same heft and shape as a deer, with the same sleek, rust-colored coat and languid, liquid, dark-chocolate eyes. Chet and I were together from 2013 to 2015. Buddy was my "true first doggie love" relationship. I learned to walk him (rather, he walked me), play with him, feed him, cuddle him, scratch him, talk to him, and adore him. And he adored me. Chet and I broke up, and I never saw Buddy again, and he—Buddy, that is—died about a year later. It's been about ten years, and while I don't miss Chet (well, every once in a while I do), my heart still aches over Buddy. And I am bereft that I did not get a chance to see my doggie sweetheart one more time before he was gone.

Rosie Wisdom
Being around people who are good for us is self-love.

Anonymous Quote
Acknowledge losses as sacred wounds.

Rosie Wisdom
Allow for your "longing heart."

Anecdote: Debi's Story—The First Father-in-Law

I met my dear girlfriend Debi D. about twelve years ago. She is a vivacious, affectionate, devoted friend, and a devout and feminist Christian (yes, devout and feminist go together); and I, of course, was, and am still, a secular Jewish feminist. Our friendship began when she became my Overeaters Anonymous sponsor. (In case you're startled and are wondering—"You? OA? Why? You're skinny!"—the answer is simple. Chocolate and other tasty treats too much and too often. Remember those twelve-step rooms I talked about? They are, indeed, safe places.) Debi and I bonded instantly and never looked back. She is the friend who always says "I love you madly, Rosie" whenever she signs off on the phone, on her Marco Polo videos, or in her text and email messages to me.

Debi's eyes lit up in relief and got a little teary with sad remembrance when we began discussing the book I was writing about disenfranchised grief. Debi has been happily married to her second husband since 2014. I know him, he's a doll. She was married and divorced for the first time when she was still in her twenties. In 2017, she learned that her first husband's father (her first father-in-law), with whom she had been very close, had recently died.

"My father-in-law was a very, very kind man. He had a PhD in electrical engineering, and his career was at the CIA doing something with satellites. I remember going with him to the CIA once and he parked in the VIP parking lot. So cool. I loved that he would mow the lawn while wearing a pith helmet; that is the most enduring picture I have of him. He taught me how to smoke cigars and drink Scotch! But mostly, he was just wonderful and kind and loving and gentle. Accepting. Encouraging. I miss him very much."

When he died, Debi grieved terribly, but she didn't feel like she had the right to, so she kept it to herself, feeling ashamed. She was relieved to tell me about this buried grief, to finally have a term for it, and to have an honored place in her heart to rest her grief *and* her love for that first father-in-law.

Rosie's Writing Exercise: LAVIE Method—
How to Live and Grieve Fully: Getting the Message

La vie means "the life" in French. This exercise helps you discover, contemplate, and practice reenfranchising your hidden griefs so that you may live *la vie—the life—*your big, full, complete, and glorious life. It is not a one-and-done type of exercise, but for whenever you notice any uncomfortable feeling such as shame, anxiety, anger, resentment, envy, or sorrow. You have permission to become curious about it and explore if there might be some unacknowledged grief somewhere below the surface that you need to tend to.

When you experience an uncomfortable feeling, observe it, contemplate it, and write about it in this way:

L Look and listen to what the emotion feels like in your body. What emotion is it? Let it speak to you. What is it saying? For instance: *I am hot, cold, tight, tingly, or sick to my stomach. Ah, I am anxiety. I am worried about getting older and might be afraid to feel sad, scared, or angry. I have an aching soreness in my heart. Ah, I am sadness and grief. My wife died and I need to cry.*

A Acknowledge, accept, and allow that the emotion is natural, normal, and human and that what it is saying is an important teaching for you. Allow the emotion and the teaching to come in and be present. For instance: *Anxiety is natural and normal. I acknowledge the anxiety, I accept and allow the anxiety to come in, and I accept what it is teaching me.*

V Validate and value the emotion and its message as you go deeper into what it is teaching you. For instance: *I am okay, and my feelings are okay. I value myself, I welcome my grief, and my self-judgment begins to melt away.*

I Investigate and integrate the emotions and messages as you go even deeper, and begin to know them as lynchpins of your core value system. For instance: *Anxiety, rage, fear, and grief are all part of being human. They help me recognize and remember what*

I believe in and what I hold most sacred; they help me claim and live according to my core value system, a value system that includes loving and honoring my aging body, my ageless spirit, and all my emotions and feelings.

E   **Engage, embrace, and enjoy** the knowledge and wisdom of your emotions and their messages. Know that you are free to celebrate, create, and revel in life—your full, fabulous, unique—and as the poet Mary Oliver describes it—"your one wild and precious life." For instance: *I allow fun, laughter, and tears—my own and those of others. I am my most joyful self and in this way, I shine my loving light on the world.*

Doing this exercise often, no matter what mood you're in, will ensure that you can hear and honor the messages your emotions are sending you. This helps you live and grieve fully and well. *L'chaim! To life!*

Wise Quote
The mortality impact of being socially disconnected is similar to that caused by smoking up to fifteen cigarettes a day.

—Dr. Vivek Murthy, US Surgeon General[77]

In other words, feeling lonely and left out is as bad for you as smoking fifteen cigarettes every single day!

Rosie Wisdom and Contemplation Exercise
The paradox about grief is that it always triggers past grief; when you grieve, all your past griefs get stirred up.

The reassuring part is that you can go back and do more healing work every time. And there will always be a theme or two or three. What's yours? And, maybe write it—or them—down.

Rosie Wisdom
Letting go does not mean not caring anymore.

Anecdote: Telly's Story—Just Good Friends in Polite Society
Telly M. is my permanent-makeup aesthetician and a talented collage artist. I could not help but adore him from the first time we met in the months before the pandemic. He can make me laugh even when he's inserting sharp needles into my face; he wears big, round, red-framed Elton John glasses and loves hugs. One day last winter, as I lay on his aesthetician's table while he inserted one of those needles gently into my almost nonexistent eyebrows, I told Telly about writing my book on disenfranchised grief. Then he told me this story.

Telly lost many friends to death during the AIDS epidemic of the 1980s and many more through the present day. For years, he hid his trauma and grief over losing these beloved ones, and he suffered additional agonizing shame and loneliness over having to conceal his own identity as a gay man. Over many years, with the support of trusted friends, family, and heart-family, Telly has been on a deeply healing journey of grieving and honoring the people he lost and his own lost years of living openly as a whole person in society. In embracing the grief and the love, Telly has learned to live and love passionately, self-compassionately, and joyfully.

"The most healing piece [in allowing the grief] has been my art, doing portraits of friends and family I have lost and being asked to do portraits of their lost loved ones," Telly explained. "It really brings it to the surface for me in a positive way. Lots of tears and joy. Thank you for writing this book, Rosie." Telly lightly dabbed a moistened, sterile mini-swab at the comely results of his handiwork. "And thanks for including my story," he said. "This type of information is so important. It explains why I held it in." We smiled at each other as he helped me sit up and handed me a mirror. "I think this ash-brown color is just perfect on you." I yelped at the now lush-browed vision of myself as he continued, "And, don't worry, the intensity of the color will calm down soon, like it always does. Just don't forget to wipe with the Aquaphor morning and night for seven days. And don't scratch!"

Rosie Wisdom

We deserve to claim all our sorrows.
Grief, loss, and death come for us all.
This fact alone is enough reason to allow ourselves
to claim and tend to our grief.

Rosie Wisdom

Acceptance and moving on from grief does not mean "getting over it."
It means carrying grief lightly and lovingly as carry-on luggage,
not burdensome baggage.

It means carrying grief with us as a sacred wound,
honoring the wound, and honoring that missing person,
animal, place, thing, or part of ourselves.

Anecdote: Patrice's Story—Anger, Yearning, and Forgiveness
Patrice is another one of my dearest, longtime Seattle girlfriends. We met in a Seattle choir in 2015 and bonded over classical hymns, Jodi Picoult, neighborhood walks, and tearjerker movie matinees at the Crest theatre. This is her story: Patrice and her four sisters were sexually abused by their father when they were teenagers. Over the years, therapy and other forms of self-care helped Patrice to accept and grieve the traumatic effects of the sexual abuse, to honor her anger, and to validate her grief and her yearning for the emotionally healthy father she did not have growing up. Years later, when she was an adult, her father, then aging, became ill, and she took care of him until his death. This was a very healing experience for Patrice. She began to forgive the father she did have, not to forgive his behavior, but to accept that he was a deeply flawed and haunted human being who needed comfort and care in his last year of life. Her ongoing journey of acknowledgment, forgiveness, and self-forgiveness has enabled her to create and nurture joy, love, deep professional satisfaction, and a sense of fun in life. The concept of disenfranchised grief has given her an added appreciation for the deep and complex strides she has made in embracing all her feelings.

Anecdote: Dr. Judy's Story—We Don't Talk Enough About Grief

About a year ago, I went in for my annual wellness visit with my primary care physician of four years, a tall, slender, striking young woman in her mid-thirties who wears her coal-black hair in a chin-length bob and black-rimmed glasses as big and round as Telly's. I love and respect my PCP, and I call her Dr. Judy. She told me I looked good, better than she remembered from our last visit more than a year before. There was something about my expression, a certain brightness in my eyes.

"Well, I have a boyfriend now," I told her. "And I'm writing a book." She was intrigued. I explained about the boyfriend and then told her about the grief memoir. Then, without prompting, she told me a disenfranchised grief story of her own, and it did not surprise me.

"When you describe disenfranchised grief, it makes me think about some patients of mine," Dr. Judy said. "Ones who have been diagnosed with a serious illness or even a terminal illness, especially young people like a twenty-five-year-old woman I worked with. They are losing their identities as healthy people, facing lives of disability, and realizing they might even die. We talk about diagnoses, prognoses, and even end-of-life care. But we don't talk about it—or call it—grief, and we don't address this grief and what to do with it! We do not talk about grief *enough* in this society. We aren't trained to think that way as doctors." I thanked her and asked if I could include her words in my book. She said of course. We hugged.

A few months later, Dr. Judy let me know she was leaving Kaiser to open her private practice where she could give her patients more individual time and attention. Damn! I was so glad for her, but so sad for myself! I am going to *miss* her. Ah, grief.

Rosie Wisdom
*Setting boundaries can bring up grief because
it so often results in someone withdrawing their love.
This is an opportunity for deep healing and self-forgiveness work.*

Rosie's Writing and Reflection Exercise: Transforming Your Grief
Write without stopping to censor or second-guess yourself; you don't need to share your words with anyone. This is just for you. But feel free to do so if it feels right and safe. Let your answers be as short or as long as you like, and feel free to come back to them often.

Choose an experience of grief about someone or something that others did or did not acknowledge and validate. (You don't have to choose the hardest example.) Then fill in the blanks:

1. When I felt grief about _____ that some people—including myself—said was not valid or appropriate, I felt _____.

2. When some people—including myself—validated and honored my grief, I felt _____.

3. This validation and honoring of my grief transformed my grief by _____.

Rosie Wisdom
Carry grief as precious cargo throughout life.

Rosie Wisdom
All feelings are valid, including feelings of grief.
They need compassionate, nonjudgmental, loving attention so that they can be understood, flow through you and out of you, be released, and then flow through you again and released again—and again and again.

Anonymous Quote
Grief is messy because life is messy.

Rosie's Writing and Reflection Exercise:
Your Very Own Disenfranchised Grief List

Sit quietly in a safe space. Focus on the losses you have experienced—people, things, or situations in your life that have been lost and have caused you pain, sorrow, angst, fear, other trauma, or discomfort that were not recognized and acknowledged as valid, real grief by yourself or others, family, friends, and society. Write these losses down on your list. These might include a person, a pet, a stuffed toy, a bad friend, a parent, a lover, a job, a special earring, your hearing, an arm or leg, your sight, or another bodily function.

Or they might include a character in a novel like Anna in *Anna Karenina*, Beth March in *Little Women*, or some other fictitious or real person you have never seen or known up close. List everything and everyone you can think of, don't hesitate, and don't overthink it. And if, at any point, this activity becomes overwhelming, take a break. It's okay.

Reflect on each one as you have the time. And, slowly begin to let yourself acknowledge them all as valid reasons to grieve. Again, you can keep these writings private, or sit with a trusted person and talk about your insights. The longer the items on this list become, the more you will understand what disenfranchised grief looks like, and that you have a right to reenfranchise it all and welcome it into your heart.

Here are some examples from my personal list:

- Volunteering on Friday evenings during the summer after my separation at a homeless shelter for young adults and coming home alone afterward with a heart full of sadness and yearning—for the husband who was no more, the child I never had, and for the sadness and yearning of these kids
- Being single
- Losing all my eldercare companion clients (my sweet "little old ladies"), their families, and their pets
- Volunteering three days a week for four months in 2012 with kids from ages eight to eighteen at an orphanage in Morelia, Mexico
- The death by suicide during the pandemic of the twentysomething son of a friend

- The death of Martin Luther King Jr.
- The death of Robert F. Kennedy
- The death of John Lennon
- The death of Tony in *West Side Story*
- The death of Leonard Bernstein
- The death of Princess Diana

You get the idea.

Wise Quote
How do I stay in the present moment when it feels unbearable?
Look deeply into the nature of your suffering…and then that energy
of mindfulness…helps you to be strong enough to recognize
and counter the pain and embrace it tenderly.[78]

Most people are afraid of suffering.
But suffering is a kind of mud to help the lotus flower of happiness grow.
There can be no lotus flower without the mud.[79]

Being able to enjoy happiness doesn't require that we have zero suffering.
In fact, the art of happiness is also the art of suffering well.
When we learn to acknowledge, embrace, and understand our suffering,
we suffer much less. Not only that, but we're also able to go further
and transform our suffering into understanding, compassion,
and joy for ourselves and for others.[80]

—Thich Nhat Hanh, Zen Buddhist monk, master, teacher,
author, peace activist, and Rosie's favorite Zen master

Rosie Wisdom
There is the phrase "friends and loved ones."
My friends are my loved ones.

Gladness Exercise: Things to Do for Fun

Hold a pencil between your teeth. It will force your lips into a smile. And if you like, look in the mirror. Once you are looking in the mirror, take out the pencil from between your teeth (or not), cross your eyes, and giggle. If you can't giggle, try snorting or hooting. Then you will probably giggle or guffaw. Crying is fine, too.

And, try other fun things like finger painting—yes, with your fingers!—or dancing like crazy, swaying, swooshing, or hopping around, or otherwise moving your body in safe, comfortable ways to your favorite rowdy or resonating music. Draw with your nondominant hand, sing off-key on purpose, or play a musical instrument you have never tried. Take a beginner art class (especially if you are not an artist!), play miniature golf, or join a nonaudition choir that sings your favorite songs or that will challenge you with ones you don't know so well. Climb a tree that is easy to climb and that won't hurt you if you fall out of it. Jump on a trampoline, float in a pool or the ocean, or run through a water sprinkler. Blow bubbles. Pillow fight gently with a good friend and some very old pillows that nobody wants anymore.

Rosie Wisdom
Longing for love is not shameful;
it is an awesome gift to share—
you are a gift, a treasure to share.

Wise Quote
Meaning, truth, and kindness are our constant teachers.
They help us live through fear, pain, and disappointment.
They are flames that light the heart.[81]

When facing what's ours to face, we're surprised to learn, time and again,
that under what seems unbearable is the rest of life waiting to be lived.[82]

—Mark Nepo, poet, teacher, storyteller, and philosopher

Rosie Wisdom
Grief healing includes what I affectionately call my
"spiritual Alka-Seltzer for grief."

The act of allowing the grief to simply be can bring us relief
in an instant because it releases us from shame.

It does not take the grief away, but the sense of disenfranchisement
can fall away as easily as taking a mindful breath because
we are giving back to our grief its sacred status.
And then it is no longer disenfranchised.

Writing Exercise: Rainy Day Letter
The "Rainy Day Letter" exercise is adapted from Kaiser Permanente Mental Health and Wellness Recovery Group, Seattle, Washington, November 7, 2022:

Write a self-care letter to yourself that reminds you of the lovable person you are. Put it away in a safe place. Then, when the rainy day comes, take it out and read it to yourself out loud. (My adaptation goes like this: Better yet, have a dear friend—or two or three—write you a note about the lovable person they know you are, and put these notes in your safe place, too. Even better, don't put them away at all—keep them handy and read them out loud to yourself every day! It's mostly rainy every day here in Seattle, anyway!)

Wise Quote
The experience of grieving makes it clear to me that grief
does not occur in predictable stages with obvious endpoints.

It is, however, a relief to learn the famous Five Stages were not meant
to describe my grief. This means I am not doing something wrong.[83]

—Amy Lin, author

Writing Exercise: Grief Journal Writing Prompts

These grief-journal writing prompts are from Whatsyourgrief.com, a website that offers grief education, online courses, and opportunities for sharing, community, and more:[84]

1. As my grief changes, I worry that _____.
Personal example: *I worry that I will forget Kevin—what he looked like, what his voice sounded like, his goofy grin—and that would mean he was not important to me and that my grief was not valid. And that the guilt, the anger, and the question "Why did this happen?" will last forever. Or worse, that the unrelenting pain and grief will last forever.*

2. Moving forward in my grief means that _____.
Personal example: *No matter how much Kevin's face fades, I know my worries will lessen, my fears will ease, and I will be able to remember him with fondness and connection and not as much pain and devastation. And when the pain inevitably rises up, I will greet it, not with fear, but with reverence, tenderness, and appreciation. These are the proofs of my love.*

3. Ask the person who is gone this question: If I could ask you what you want for me and my future, what would you tell me?
Personal example: *Kevin's response: "I'm so sorry, Rosie. I did not mean to leave you like that. But it was my time, I guess. I couldn't help it. I did keep my promise to you, though, I lived with you for the rest of my life here on Earth! I see how grief-stricken you are, so just remember what a creative, full life you have, with fun and meaningful goals. You can carry my memory with you every day, wherever you are and whatever you accomplish. I'm right here with you. Don't forget."*

Rosie Wisdom
Be kind and set good limits.

Rosie Wisdom
Complicated grief can simply mean lots of it, all at once.

Wise Quote
We are not human beings having a spiritual experience.
We are spiritual beings having a human experience.

—Attributed to Pierre Teilhard de Chardin,
twentieth-century philosopher and mystic

Things to Do with Grief
Here are Nikki Moberly's "five steps to help cope with disenfranchised grief":[85]

1. Learn about grief.
2. Find your support systems.
3. Ask for what you need.
4. Create a specific ritual to honor your loss.
5. Know when to ask for help.

More Things to Do with Grief
In the WebMD article, "What to Know About Disenfranchised Grief," Smitha Bhandari, MD, summarizes two general opportunities for helping heal from disenfranchised grief and all grief. I agree:

Therapy. One-on-one talk therapy and support groups can help you understand and accept a loss. Therapists can provide a helpful outside perspective to your internal feelings.

Personal work. On your own, you can work to build thought patterns and coping methods that help you heal from grief. Let yourself feel your feelings without judgment. You can express your feelings through journaling, talking to trusted friends, art, or other outlets.

You can also create your own rituals or traditions to recognize a loss. Observing an anniversary or birthday, visiting a grave, or keeping a deceased person's items can help you process a loss.[86]

One More Thing to Do with Grief
Rosie's favorite, worth repeating over and over again: Find a therapist who suits you!

Wise Quote
We grieve because we love. Grief is part of love.
There was love in this world before your loss,
there is love surrounding you now, and love will remain beside you,
through all the life that is yet to come.
The forms will change, but love itself will never leave.
It's not enough. And it's everything.[87]

—Megan Devine, psychotherapist, speaker, trainer,
podcaster, and author

Rosie Wisdom
Consistent, loving attention and healthy hugs can be lifesaving.

Rosie Wisdom
On having a therapist and what it means to me:

Without a therapist—a guiding friend—I sometimes feel adrift in a tiny,
slowly leaking boat in a vast, gray, roiling ocean with nowhere to land,
nowhere to rest, nothing to grasp onto, to feel anchored and supported.

I am alone and lonely and lost. But with a therapist, we are together
and our boat is seaworthy; sometimes the water is calm,
sometimes we are adrift; sometimes we move through rough waters,
and sometimes through smooth waters, but moving together, connected.

Rowing, resting, moored, occasionally almost capsizing, yet we are
still moving, upright, and calm, no matter how rocky the waves.

Final Reminders

So, dear reader, have fun on the road. Remember as you set out or continue on your way: Pack protein snacks, water, an apple, an avocado, or another healthful fruit, and a few chocolates or other delectable treats if allowed. Take bathroom breaks, stretch breaks, nap breaks, and healthful meal breaks. Try to get a good night's sleep each night. And, at least once a day, call someone you love. Do not text. Call.

I Hold You in My Heart—
a Daily Practice

My dear friend, Susanne, often says, "I hold you in my heart" when she expresses her love for me, not only when I'm in pain, but all the time. What exquisite and rapturous words they are. She's not trying to fix anything or distract me from my pain or my grief when I'm hurting. She is offering me a heart space—a heart place—where I can rest, where I can feel love and pain, where I can heal, and where I can simply be.

Daily Practice: *To Kevin, to Sadie, and all the loves of my life whom I have adored and lost through death or some other way: I hold you in my heart, the essence of you, the memory of you, my love for you, and my grief over you. I hold you, and I hold my grief, tenderly and lightly, and as a sacred honoring of us.*

To all the loves of and in my life who are gone from me or from this world, to whom it has been harder for me to love and forgive: *I hold you in my heart, my love for you, my grief and all my feelings for you, and my efforts toward forgiving you and myself. I do this as a daily reminder, with tenderness, affirmation, compassion, and self-compassion.*

And, to me: *I hold myself in my own heart, to remember my lovability and my ability to love and to forgive myself and others. I call up my values and vulnerability, my healthy boundaries, physical and emotional, the image of my worth, and my right to grieve all my losses. I do this as a daily reminder, with tenderness, self-compassion, and unconditional regard.* (I often forget these mantras—more often than I would like to admit—but I do my best. This is why such reverential holding is called daily practice—so we can try to practice and remind ourselves every day—so that we don't forget.)

This is how I am learning to live through, with, and beyond loss and grief.

Thus, dear reader, be without shame with your grief. To claim it is your right, your privilege as a human being, your responsibility to yourself, and a gift to those you cherish. Who knows? You might be a catalyst for this new kind of generational gift-giving—the gift of honoring and allowing, of embracing and reenfranchising your disenfranchised grief. I believe this is helping change the world, a little bit at a time, one griever at a time. Claim your grief mindfully, tenderly, and self-compassionately. Allow yourself to be soothed by your whole imperfect self, by your own broken heart, and by those vital loving witnesses who will see it, see you, and see it through with you.

It is not easy. And it is ongoing. But it is enough. And it is *everything*. This claiming—this embracing of our grief—holds us in the arms of love as we live our lives deeply and fully—as we live *la vie—the complete life*—and as we grieve all our sorrows, big, small, and everything in between.

Notes

Introduction

1   Kenneth J. Doka, "Disenfranchised Grief: Dr. Ken Doka," interview, October 4, 2013, Springer Publishing Company, YouTube, 5 min., 25 sec., https://www.youtube.com/watch?v=BhfxzY65SmI.

2   *Merriam-Webster Unabridged Dictionary*, "shame," accessed September 25, 2025, https//www.merriam-webster.com/dictionary/shame.

Chapter Five: Life After Kevin

3   Kenneth J. Doka, "Disenfranchised Grief: Dr. Ken Doka," interview, October 4, 2013, Springer Publishing Company, YouTube, 5 min., 25 sec., https://www.youtube.com/watch?v=BhfxzY65SmI.

Chapter Ten: Words from the Experts

4   Kenneth J. Doka, "Introduction," in *Disenfranchised Grief: Recognizing Hidden Sorrow* (Lexington Books, 1989), xv.

5   Doka, "Disenfranchised Grief," in *Disenfranchised Grief*, 4.

6   Doka, "Introduction," in *Disenfranchised Grief*, xvi.

7   *Merriam Webster's Collegiate Dictionary*, 11th ed. (2019), under "acknowledge."

8   *Merriam Webster's Collegiate Dictionary*, 11th ed. (2019), under "bereavement."

9   *Merriam Webster's Collegiate Dictionary*, 11th ed. (2019), under "disenfranchise."

10   Doka, "Introduction," in *Disenfranchised Grief*, xvi.

11   *Merriam Webster's Collegiate Dictionary*, 11th ed. (2019), under "grief."

12   *Merriam Webster's Collegiate Dictionary*, 11th ed. (2019), under "grieve."

13   *Merriam Webster's Collegiate Dictionary*, 11th ed. (2019), under "improper."

14 *Merriam Webster's Collegiate Dictionary*, 11th ed. (2019), under "impropriety."

15 *Merriam Webster's Collegiate Dictionary*, 11th ed. (2019), under "loss."

16 *Merriam Webster's Collegiate Dictionary*, 11th ed. (2019), under "shame."

17 *Merriam Webster's Collegiate Dictionary*, 11th ed. (2019), under "validate."

18 "Meet Lisa Zoll," Grief Relief, LLC, accessed September 9, 2025, https://griefrelief-therapy.com/about/staff/lisa-zoll/.

19 "Meet Lisa Zoll," Grief Relief, LLC.

20 Lisa S. Zoll, "Disenfranchised Grief: When Grief and Grievers Are Unrecognized," *The New Social Worker: The Social Work Careers Magazine*, Winter 2019, https://www.socialworker.com/feature-articles/practice/disenfranchised-grief-when-grief-and-grievers-are-unrecogniz/.

21 Zoll, "Disenfranchised Grief."

22 Zoll, "Disenfranchised Grief."

23 Zoll, "Disenfranchised Grief."

24 Doka, "Disenfranchised Grief," in *Disenfranchised Grief,* 4–7.

25 Zoll, "Disenfranchised Grief."

26 Zoll, "Disenfranchised Grief."

27 Amazon.com, "About the Author" description of Lynn Shiner, author of *Stabbed in the Heart: Three Murdered Children, Two Resilient Mothers*, accessed September 9, 2025, https://www.amazon.com/stores/author/B00RQXCTEO/about?ccs_id=e-02fe30e-6c62-4fee-863d-e047c944032f.

28 Zoll, "Disenfranchised Grief."

29 Zoll, "Disenfranchised Grief."

30 Zoll, "Disenfranchised Grief."

31 Zoll, "Disenfranchised Grief."

32 Nikki Moberly, "Coping with Disenfranchised Grief: Five Steps to Start Healing," BetterUp.com, December 14, 2021, https://www.betterup.com/blog/disenfranchised-grief.

33 Moberly, "Coping with Disenfranchised Grief."

34 Moberly, "Coping with Disenfranchised Grief."

35 Moberly, "Coping with Disenfranchised Grief."

36 Moberly, "Coping with Disenfranchised Grief."

37 Moberly, "Coping with Disenfranchised Grief."

38 Moberly, "Coping with Disenfranchised Grief."

39 Moberly, "Coping with Disenfranchised Grief."

40   Smitha Bhandari, MD, and WebMD Editorial Contributors, "What to Know About Disenfranchised Grief," WebMD, February 25, 2024, https://www.webmd.com/mental-health/what-to-know-about-disenfranchised-grief.

41   Bhandari, "What to Know About Disenfranchised Grief."

Chapter Eleven: Our Society's Mandate Games for Grief

42   Kenneth J. Doka, "Disenfranchised Grief," in *Disenfranchised Grief: Recognizing Hidden Sorrow* (Lexington Books, 1989), 4.

43   Elisabeth Kübler-Ross, chap. 3–7 in *On Death and Dying: What the Dying Have to Teach Doctors, Nurses, Clergy & Their Own Families* (Simon & Schuster, 1969).

44   Ira Byock, "Foreword," in *On Death and Dying: What the Dying Have to Teach Doctors, Nurses, Clergy & Their Own Families*, Elizabeth Kübler-Ross (Scribner, 2014), xiii.

45   Byock, *On Death and Dying*, xiv.

Chapter Twelve: More Antidotes

46   Nikki Moberly, "Coping with Disenfranchised Grief: Five Steps to Start Healing," BetterUp.com, December 14, 2021, https://www.betterup.com/blog/disenfranchised-grief.

47   Moberly, "Coping with Disenfranchised Grief."

48   Francis Weller, "The Five Gates of Grief," in *The Wild Edge of Sorrow: Rituals of Renewal and the Sacred Work of Grief* (North Atlantic Books, 2015), 46.

49   Weller, "The Five Gates of Grief," in *The Wild Edge of Sorrow*, 24–69.

50   Weller, "The Five Gates of Grief," in *The Wild Edge of Sorrow*, 31.

51   Weller, "The Five Gates of Grief," in *The Wild Edge of Sorrow*, 63.

52   Weller, "Introduction," in *The Wild Edge of Sorrow*, xx.

53   Weller, "Introduction," in *The Wild Edge of Sorrow*, xviii–xix.

54   Weller, "Introduction," in *The Wild Edge of Sorrow*, xix.

55   Weller, "Introduction," in *The Wild Edge of Sorrow*, xxi.

56   Weller, "Introduction," in *The Wild Edge of Sorrow*, xxi.

57   Weller, "Introduction," in *The Wild Edge of Sorrow*, xxii.

58   Weller, "Introduction," in *The Wild Edge of Sorrow*, xxii–xxiii.

59   Weller, "Introduction," in *The Wild Edge of Sorrow*, xxiii.

60   David Kessler, "Mother's Day Grief: When You're Grieving Mom," online webcast, May 9, 2023, 1 hour, 6 min., https://www.davidkesslertraining.com/mothers-day-grief-replay-mother.

61   Kessler, "Mother's Day Grief."

62   Kessler, "Mother's Day Grief."

Chapter Thirteen: Banished

63   *Merriam Webster's Collegiate Dictionary*, 11th ed. (2019), under "banish."

64   William Shakespeare, *The Tragedy of Romeo and Juliet*, ed. Barbara Mowat, Paul Werstine, Michael Poston, Rebecca Niles, (Folger Shakespeare Library, n.d.), accessed September 9, 2025, https://www.folger.edu/explore/shakespeares-works/romeo-and-juliet/read/.

Chapter Fifteen: The Broken Heart Syndrome

65   Torah: What observant Jews call the first five chapters of the Old Testament. These were the books believed to have been written by Moses.

66   Mayo Clinic staff, "Broken Heart Syndrome," November 11, 2023, https://www.mayoclinic.org/diseases-conditions/broken-heart-syndrome/symptoms-causes/syc-20354617.

67   *Merriam Webster's Collegiate Dictionary*, 11th ed. (2019), under "eye-rolling."

68   Wikipedia, "eye-rolling," last modified May 16, 2025, 15:03 (UTC), https://en.wikipedia.org/wiki/Eye-rolling.

69   whokeepsthisstuff, "Del Webb's Sun City Brochure," Etsy.com, accessed September 9, 2025, https://www.etsy.com/listing/1392453982/del-webbs-sun-city-brochure?-show_sold_out_detail=1&ref=nla_listing_details.

Chapter Sixteen: A Different Heartstring

70   Based on the 1957 book by Dodie Smith, *The Hundred and One Dalmatians*, by Viking Press.

71   Gateway Services, Inc., *Coping with the Loss of a Companion Animal: Support Guide for Families*, June 2019, https://vcparker.net/wp-content/uploads/2022/06/Gateway-Grief-Support-Resource-Book-June-2019.pdf.

Chapter Seventeen: For the Love of Pets

72   Sarah Hoggan, "Pet Loss Grief: The Pain Explained." TEDx Talks, Temecula, Calif., November 10, 2022, 16 min., 39 sec., https://www.youtube.com/watch?v=TkJGh-QANjZo.

73   Sarah Hoggan, "Pet Loss Grief."

74   Sarah Hoggan, "Pet Loss Grief."

75 Sarah Hoggan, "Pet Loss Grief."

76 Not One More Vet, "Our Story & Mission," NOMV.org, accessed September 9, 2025, https://nomv.org/our-story-and-mission/.

Chapter Eighteen: Inside the Road Map

77 Dr. Vivek Murthy, *Our Epidemic of Loneliness and Isolation: The US Surgeon General's Advisory on the Healing Effects of Social Connection and Community* (Office of the US Surgeon General, 2023), 4.

78 Thich Nhat Hanh, "How Do I Stay in the Present Moment When It Feels Unbearable?," Plum Village, May 29, 2014, YouTube, 0:19–0:24, 6:43–6:46, and 6:56–7:08, https://www.youtube.com/watch?v=t5Ka2RS0UC4.

79 Thich Nhat Hanh, *No Mud, No Lotus: The Art of Transforming Suffering* (Parallax Press, 2014), v.

80 Thich Nhat Hanh, "The Art of Transforming Suffering," in *No Mud, No Lotus: The Art of Transforming Suffering* (Parallax Press, 2014), 10.

81 Mark Nepo, "Living with Meaning, Truth, and Kindness," in *The Book of Soul: 52 Paths to Living What Matters* (St. Martin's Essentials, 2020), 5.

82 Mark Nepo, "Where All Souls Meet," in *The Book of Soul: 52 Paths to Living What Matters* (St. Martin's Essentials, 2020), xv.

83 Amy Lin, *Here After: A Memoir* (Zibby, 2024), 106.

84 What's Your Grief, accessed September 9, 2025, https://whatsyourgrief.com/product/lessons-to-write-on-a-guided-grief-journaling-intensive-ebook-edition/.

85 Nikki Moberly, "Coping with Disenfranchised Grief: Five Steps to Start Healing," BetterUp.com, December 14, 2021, https://www.betterup.com/blog/disenfranchised-grief.

86 Smitha Bhandari, MD, and WebMD Editorial Contributors, "What to Know About Disenfranchised Grief," WebMD, February 25, 2024, https://www.webmd.com/mental-health/what-to-know-about-disenfranchised-grief.

87 Megan Devine, "Love Is the Only Thing That Lasts," in *It's OK That You're Not OK: Meeting Grief and Loss in a Culture That Doesn't Understand* (Sounds True, 2017), 229.

BOOKS

Being Present for Grievers

Being There for Someone in Grief: Essential Lessons for Supporting Someone Grieving from Death, Loss, and Trauma, Marianna Cacciatore, Raku Press, 2010.

It's OK That You're Not OK: Meeting Grief and Loss in a Culture That Doesn't Understand, Megan Devine, Sounds True, 2017. (See the appendix titled "How to Help a Grieving Friend," pages 237–241.)

The Art of Comforting: What to Say and Do for People in Distress, Val Walker, Tarcher, 2010.

Healing a Friend's Grieving Heart: 100 Practical Ideas for Helping Someone You Love Through Loss, Alan D. Wolfelt, Companion Press, 2001. (Companion Press is the publishing imprint of the Center for Loss and Life Transition and specializes in resources for grief education and support.)

Child Loss

Comfort: A Journey Through Grief, Ann Hood, W. W. Norton & Company, 2008.

The Disappearance: A Primer of Loss, Geneviève Jurgensen, W. W. Norton & Company, 2000.

Memoirs

What Looks like Bravery: An Epic Journey Through Loss to Love, Laurel Braitman, Simon & Schuster, 2023.

Grief Is for People, Sloane Crosley, MCD Books, 2024.

The Year of Magical Thinking, Joan Didion, Vintage Books, 2007.

Bits and Pieces: My Mother, My Brother, and Me, Whoopi Goldberg, Blackstone Publishing, 2024.

Grief Is Love: Living with Loss, Marisa Renee Lee, Legacy Lit Books, 2022.

Here After: A Memoir, Amy Lin, Zibby Books, 2024.

A Three Dog Life, Abigail Thomas, Harcourt, 2006.

Pet Loss

Lost Companions: Reflections on the Death of Pets, Jeffrey Moussaieff Masson, St. Martin's Press, 2020.

Alex and Me: How a Scientist and a Parrot Discovered a Hidden World of Animal Intelligence—and Formed a Deep Bond in the Process, Irene Pepperberg, HarperCollins, 2008.

Scholarly Books

Children Mourning, Mourning Children, Kenneth J. Doka, editor, Taylor & Francis, 1995.

Disenfranchised Grief: Recognizing Hidden Sorrow, Kenneth J. Doka, editor, Lexington Books, 1989.

Grief Is a Journey: Finding Your Path Through Loss, Kenneth J. Doka, Atria Books, 2016.

On Death and Dying: What the Dying Have to Teach Doctors, Nurses, Clergy and Their Own Families, Elisabeth Kübler-Ross, Scribner, 1969.

Self-Help
Bearing the Unbearable: Love, Loss, and the Heartbreaking Path of Grief, Joanne Cacciatore, Wisdom Publications, 2017.

It's OK That You're Not OK: Meeting Grief and Loss in a Culture That Doesn't Understand, Megan Devine, Sounds True, 2017.

A Guide to Grief, Cole Imperi (author) and Bianca Jagoe (illustrator), Kids Can Press, 2024. (For juveniles.)

Losing a Parent: Passage to a New Way of Living: A Guide to Facing Death and Dying, Alexandra Kennedy, HarperSanFrancisco, 1991.

Finding Meaning: The Sixth Stage of Grief, David Kessler, Scribner, 2019.

How to Go On Living When Someone You Love Dies, Therese A. Rando, Bantam Books, 1991.

Invisible Loss: Recognizing and Healing the Unacknowledged Heartbreak of Everyday Grief, Christina Rasmussen, Sounds True, 2024.

Anxiety: The Missing Stage of Grief: A Revolutionary Approach to Understanding and Healing the Impact of Loss, Claire Bidwell Smith, Balance, 2020.

The Wild Edge of Sorrow: Rituals of Renewal and the Sacred Work of Grief, Francis Weller, North Atlantic Books, 2015.

Workbooks
How to Carry What Can't Be Fixed: A Journal for Grief, Megan Devine, Sounds True, 2021.

The Grief Recovery Handbook: The Action Program for Moving Beyond Death, Divorce, and Other Losses: 20th Anniversary Expanded Edition, John W. James and Russell Friedman, William Morrow Paperbacks, 2017.

Navigating Grief: A Guided Journal: Prompts and Exercises for Reflection and Healing, Mia Roldan, Callisto, 2021.

ONLINE RESOURCES AND PODCASTS

Anderson Cooper
All There Is with Anderson Cooper
cnn.com/audio/podcasts/all-there-is-with-anderson-cooper
In this podcast, Anderson Cooper reflects on grief and loss and discusses with his guests their grief and loss stories. Debuted in 2022.

David Kessler
grief.com
davidkesslertraining.com
Grief.com is a website created by David Kessler with professional support, books, articles, and other educational materials about healing grief. Davidkesslertraining.com is the home of Tender Hearts, an online, general-loss grief-support community led by David Kessler, plus smaller loss-specific groups.

Death, Grief, and Belief
deathgriefandbelief.com

Death, Grief, and Belief is a consortium of educators whose mission is to create a safe space for unpacking religious beliefs and spiritual concepts that can be disempowering and harmful when one is facing loss, trauma, death, and bereavement.

For Grief
Forgrief.com

For Grief offers extensive, collaborative grief support and resilience resources, including videos of chats with grief experts; a huge library of books, videos, and other resources; courses; a speakers bureau; online gatherings; a monthly newsletter called *Mourning Boost*; a blog; and a Facebook community.

Refuge in Grief
refugeingrief.com

Grief expert and psychotherapist Megan Devine's website provides clinical training, certificate programs, and encouragement for healthcare workers, leaders, and other professionals as well as grievers and their supporters. It also offers a library of videos, articles, other resources, and the *It's OK That You're Not OK* podcast.

Reimagine
letsreimagine.org

Reimagine's mission is "to help all people face adversity, loss, and mortality, and channel the hard parts of life into meaningful action and growth." It hosts virtual events, grief groups, and coping-skills workshops and retreats, and it offers grief literature, articles, and other resources.

What's Your Grief
whatsyourgrief.com

What's Your Grief offers grief support and education, including comprehensive information about grief and bereavement. As a place for sharing, support, resources, and more, it covers various types of loss, coping mechanisms, and the grieving process in general. It also includes a podcast, articles, courses, membership communities, and its book, *What's Your Grief: Lists to Help You Through Any Loss.*

Wild Grief
wildgrief.org
Wild Grief is a nonprofit organization based in Olympia, Washington, that provides "free peer support programs in nature to grieving youth, families, and people of all ages. We combine peer-based grief support with the healing power of nature."

Wild Heart
wildheart.space
Founded by author and teacher Mirabai Starr and interspiritual practitioner, facilitator, and artist Willow Brook, Wild Heart offers "a tender refuge and a guiding hand as you courageously engage in dismantling false belief structures and embrace a more conscious life, expanding your capacity to be transformed by the inevitable losses life brings." Wild Heart offers in-person and online retreats and other events, individual support, and *The Wild Heart* podcast.

Your Morbid Friends
yourmorbidfriends.com
Founded and run by Cassandra Biron, LCSW, and Robin Silver, MA, YMF's mission "as your morbid friends is to help foster a culture of grief and death literacy through experiential psychoeducation, ritual, and community." The website's resources include in-person and online events, services, book recommendations, courses, and worksheets.

Permission to quote and discuss the following material has been graciously granted by authors and rightsholders:

Excerpts from *Disenfranchised Grief: Recognizing Hidden Sorrow* by Kenneth J. Doka, 1989, Lexington Books. Used with permission from Kenneth Doka.

Excerpts from "Disenfranchised Grief: When Grief and Grievers Are Unrecognized" by Lisa S. Zoll, Winter 2019, *The New Social Worker: The Social Work Careers Magazine*. Used with permission from Lisa S. Zoll.

Excerpts from "Coping with Disenfranchised Grief: Five Steps to Start Healing" by Nikki Moberly, December 14, 2021, BetterUp.com. Used with permission from Nikki Moberly and BetterUp Content Usage team at BetterUp.com.

Excerpts from "What to Know About Disenfranchised Grief" by Smitha Bhandari, MD, and WebMD editorial contributors, February 25, 2024, WebMD. Used with permission from WebMD.

Excerpts from "Foreword" by Ira Byock in *On Death and Dying: What the Dying Have to Teach Doctors, Nurses, Clergy and Their Own Families* by Elisabeth Kübler-Ross, 2014, Scribner. Used with permission from Ira Byock, MD.

Excerpts from *The Wild Edge of Sorrow: Rituals of Renewal and the Sacred Work of Grief* by Francis Weller, 2015, North Atlantic Books. Used with permission from Francis Weller.

Quotes from "Mother's Day Grief: When You're Grieving Mom" by David Kessler, May 9, 2023. Used with permission from Tracy@Team David Kessler.

Quotes from "Pet Loss Grief: The Pain Explained" by Sarah Hoggan, November 10, 2022, TEDx Talks. Used with permission from Sarah Hoggan.

Excerpts from "What's Your Grief" journaling course, accessed September 2025, Whatsyourgrief.com. Used with permission from Mary Manera, Grief Services Coordinator, Whatsyourgrief.com.

ACKNOWLEDGMENTS

My deepest thanks to Kevin's parents, George and Ann, and to Kevin's brother Ian, who told me he knew I would tell the story with love.

To Bill Phillips, Kevin's boss, who open-heartedly welcomed the Boggs men and me to experience Kevin at work and blessed the story with his approval.

To Betty, my friend, colleague, and mentor in all things related to love, lifelong learning, and creativity, since our days as young social workers at Catholic Charities in Brockton, Massachusetts, beginning over forty years ago. You and your writing have been my inspiration for thinking I had something to say to the world and the ability to write it all down.

To Ami, artist, friend, soul sister, you lit the match for the "essential roomie" underneath me, and fanned those embers into flames for me to carry it through and make it a book. Thanks for permitting me to share your part of my story in these pages.

To all my additional devoted and trusted readers—Terry, Susanne, Peggy, Barb S, Mary Jean, Joanne, Debi L, Andi, Dr. Judy, Dr. D, Dr. Lisa, Ahuvah, Mary B, Jeri and Richard, Terry E, Heidi Ricci, cousins Sharon and Lisa Wigutoff, and all the others who read, listened to, reflected on, responded to, suggested, encouraged, supported, and applauded my pages all along the way.

To everyone who shared and entrusted me with your own grief stories for inclusion in the book as it unfolded.

To all the authors, scholars, and other grief experts and creators from whom I gleaned knowledge, support, and guidance in my grief journey, this writing journey, and in learning and understanding what disenfranchised is and why it matters; you permitted me to use your wise words in the book. I am grateful to Amelia Carroll, LMHC, CT, SD, for her thoughtful insights, knowledge, contributions, and enthusiastic guidance during the initial phases of creating this memoir.

To the Punchy Books Accelerator writing course, taught by Matt Rudnitsky, which helped me discover the story inside me that might indeed have a message for other people, and gave me the confidence to go for it; to my badass writing accountability buddy, Jen Huerta, whom I met in the course—we bonded like Gorilla Glue and have been every-other-week accountability accomplices for over three years now; and to my Women Writing Memoirs Zoom Group, an offshoot of the PBA writing course, especially the group leader Sabrina for her support and belief in me.

To Tracy and Robin, my two grief buddies whom I met in my six-week grief support group and who embraced and supported me in my grief over Kevin, in writing this book and who have become heart family; and to Meredith Deaton, our grief support group leader and grief counselor who saw my grief and supported its validity.

To Terry, Peggy, and Mary Jean, my Seattle Wisdom Circle of Three, whose insight and dedication have helped me polish this book from its first rough-edged drafts to its final shine.

To Carly Catt and Jordan at Catt Editing, my first editing team, solid, strong, dedicated supporters when I was a newbie know-nothing as a writer, who kept reminding me this book was well-written and much needed.

To Mi Ae Lipe, my editor, self-publishing consultant, mentor, and guru who has been my rock to the last em dash and beyond.

To Sadie, Sweet Pea, and Cruella De Vil, my furry children. You are the other sweet, sacred heartstrings that are woven throughout this never-ending love story. I miss you, and I love you.

And to Michael, who listened to all of it.

Norma "Rosie" Wigutoff hails from Ketchikan, Alaska, and grew up in Annandale, Virginia, outside of Washington, DC. She received her bachelor's degree in psychology from American University and her master's in social work from Boston University. She has been a hospital social worker, a protective services caseworker, a matchmaker at the Big Brothers Big Sisters of Boston, Massachusetts, and a therapist in private practice in Boston and Seattle.

She has also been a photographer, a trap set drummer, a private therapeutic eldercare companion, and an editor. She has raised three cat children from kittenhood and cat adolescence through the end of their nine lives.

Rosie continues to learn about grief, loss, and love every day. This is her first book.

www.ingramcontent.com/pod-product-compliance
Lightning Source LLC
Chambersburg PA
CBHW051308120626
46547CB00015B/2145